Yer O

Dialect po
Welsh and English from Cymru

Edited by
Mike Jenkins

Go back into the world below the hill,
The world of food and clothes, and troubled rest,
And broken hearts, and all the common cares
Of all the common days and nights...

—Idris Davies, 'Beyond the Black Tips'

CULTURE MATTERS

First published 2023 by **Culture Matters.**
Culture Matters promotes cultural democracy.
See www.culturematters.org.uk

Layout and typesetting by Alan Morrison

ISBN: 978-1-912710-54-6

Acknowledgements

Many thanks to the Books Council of Wales for financial support for this project.

Diolch yn fawr i Gyngor Llyfrau Cymru am gefnogaeth ariannol i'r prosiect hwn.

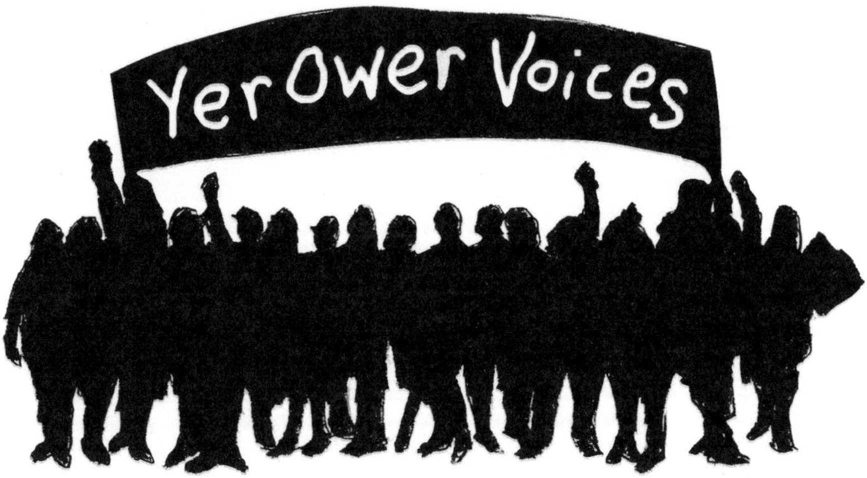

Contents

Iawn Cont?—North & West Wales

Preface

By John Barnie

Dialect poetry has had a chequered history in English. Usually these days it is looked on as a vehicle for light verse, 'inherently amusing', as David Hughes says.

It was not always so. In the fourteenth century poets writing in the West Midlands dialect wrote poems of great seriousness and subtlety. Long poems such as the anonymous *Sir Gawain and the Green Knight* and William Langland's *Piers Plowman* rivalled the court poetry of Chaucer and John Gower. It was Chaucer's southern dialect which won out, however, segueing into the 'Standard English' of later centuries. Poetry in dialect was the loser, becoming a backwater of English verse.

In Scotland it was otherwise. Scots, essentially a dialect of Middle English, became in effect a national poetic language. From Henryson and Dunbar in the late fifteenth century, through Robert Burns, to Hugh MacDiarmid and beyond, it has been the vehicle for a wide range of poetry from the amusing to the deadly serious.

What about Wales? Welsh was of course the dominant literary language for several centuries, which has complicated the situation here. Moreover, Welsh is still 'yma o hyd' so that we have the richness of two languages running side by side. English-language poets have at times used this to their advantage, appropriating Welsh forms such as the englyn.

My sense, though, is that the *dialects* of Welsh English have not been drawn on to the same degree, influenced by the Anglo conviction that dialect is not a suitable vehicle for serious poetry. The poets in this anthology disagree—dialect poetry may at one level be parochial but at its best it can, in David Hughes's formulation, be universal as well. In this sense, too, it gives voice to whole communities in Wales who may have been represented in fiction but have been invisible in the landscape of poetry.

One problem, as several contributors point out, is that there is no agreed system of spelling for Welsh-English dialects, so poets have to build from the ground up, as it were, creating their own orthographies. What is remarkable is that poets writing out of Valleys, Swansea, or Cardiff English do actually converge on the same, or very similar, written forms.

So far as I am aware, the anthology is unique in its presentation of the variety of dialect poetry written in Wales today. Unique, too, in the space it gives to poems written in dialects of Welsh, with outriders like the Guyanese creole of Maggie Harris, which has been translated into Welsh by Menna Elfyn. A notable feature of many of the poems, in fact, is the way in which the poets are aware of Welsh. Some come from Welsh, or partially recovered Welsh, backgrounds and there is often an interplay between the languages which is inventive and invigorating.

Yer Ower Voices! is pioneering, establishing dialect poetry as a genre to be taken seriously. We will, I hope, hear and read a lot more of it from now on.

Introduction

By Mike Jenkins

One of the inspirations for *Yer Ower Voices!* was taking part in the Radio 4 programme *Wales: Tongue & Talk* presented by actor Rakie Ayola. Like 'Swonzee' dialect poet David Hughes I was delighted to be included, but ultimately felt disappointed with the outcome. It portrayed our dialect work as merely humorous, even to the point of frivolity, and this is not the reality.

So I began searching out poetry which expressed so much more, about the lives of working-class people in particular, political situations which totally devalue them, and the ways in which the ever-changing language of the streets express these themes.

Humour, especially satire, can have very serious undertones and the radio programme only touched on this aspect, being more concerned with the peculiarities of language, which are constantly changing.

The other main motivation has been that no such anthology has been done before. Hopefully, it will be repeated purely in the Welsh language, which now has so much fascinating prose and poetry in the many dialects of our nation. There was space for just a few examples in this anthology.

I started by contacting a few poets who write (or have written) dialect poetry, including lloyd robson (living for some time in the United States), Gemma June Howell, Tôpher Mills, Stephen Knight and David Hughes.

Then through emails, Twitter and Facebook many more emerged. Some, such as Leigh Manley and Mary Kaye, were spurred on to write dialect poetry for the very first time, and there is a 'wild card' in Phil Knight's funny, eccentric poem.

It's interesting to see how Valleys' dialects differ and I've always been conscious of this when greeted by the brilliant Tredegar-born writer Chris Meredith with 'Ow be?' This is unheard of just down the road in my own Merthyr.

Gemma June Howell's poems sometimes read like a crossover between Cardiff and the Valleys, reflecting not only the geographical location of Caerffili, but the number of city people who have moved there.

It's exciting to include a number of Welsh language poets who examine the importance of dialect itself, and the mixture of English and Welsh in border towns like Wrecsam, with Sara Wheeler's look at the impact of dialect itself and Aled Lewis Evans's humorous combinations of Welsh and English in the voices of young people.

It's also intriguing to note the occasionally stark differences between writers from the same city: between Mab Jones and Peter Finch's 'Kerdif' and Tôpher Mills' 'Kaaaaaaairdiff', which is closer to my ear (or 'yer' in the Valleys!). Also, the way in which poets from the same city can differ greatly, as in Brian Phillips and Stephen Knight, both exiles from their Swansea home.

Like myself, Peter Akunwunmi in Newport, has arrived as an 'outsider' and often a particular dialect can be heightened in such circumstances.

Degrees of phoneticism are bound to be a challenge for anyone writing in dialect and I wonder how many choose not to make the language as phonetic as that of Stephen Knight, or simply want to suggest an accent and not imitate.

For me, this poetry lends itself to dramatic monologue and conversations and even when I take my own 'voice' it is necessarily 'other', as I don't talk like a Merthyr inhabitant despite having lived here since 1979.

Some places in Cymru have their own unique dialect and Caernarfon's 'Cofi' is just that. It's astonishing to think how the single word 'cont' (from that town) has been used so widely by Welsh social media, though not always in the way intended.

I believe dialect writing is about creating a whole world of language, much like Anthony Burgess in *A Clockwork Orange*, but one which can be both vibrant and rebellious or insulting and prejudiced.

I grew up reading working-class literature by Stan Barstow, Alan Sillitoe and Barry Hines—all male, socialist and rooted in northern England. In this anthology there's a much wider sweep: from Pete Akinwunmi, who grew up in Aberdare as the only black kid in town, to Gemma June Howell whose background was in a rough, tough Council estate in Caerffili. Maggie Harris's use of Creole is fascinating, because it feels like a full circle—a number of us were inspired by Caribbean writers such as Derek Walcott.

The title was problematic. I considered others like 'Jess Like Ewan Me' and 'Remaaaaaarkabul', ultimately deciding on one that I made up, not lifted from the poems and which could apply to many different places. The other options now head each section.

Putting 'Yer Ower Voices!' together, after my aging pc kept berating me for spelling and grammatical errors, felt like a triumph. Voices of the streets rising up, joining the Word Revolution!

Ta very much t all-a contribewters an t Mike Quille at Culture Matters f bein the Main Marn as ever.

Jess Like Ewan Me!

—Swansea

David Hughes

I was born in the Rhymney valley but have spent most of my life living in Swansea. I write 'conventionally' but have also been writing Swansea dialect poetry since the mid-eighties.

I write in dialect for two main reasons. Firstly I enjoy the challenge of trying to replicate the way people speak. We all run words together when we talk and have distinctive intonations and pronunciation, but conventional written recording does not allow you to reflect this. Secondly I believe all languages (indeed all means of communication) are precious and 'received pronunciation' or any notions of 'correctness' should not be used to exclude people or minimise their feelings, opinions or mode of expression.

In the mid-eighties Nigel Jenkins introduced me to the work of Tom Leonard, the Scottish poet who had been writing in Glasgow dialect since the late sixties. I was greatly impressed with his work. His seven poems 'Unrelated incidents' remain particularly relevant to issues of language and class. Around the same time, Nigel showed me some of the poetry of Irene Thomas, the poet from Ebbw Vale. Her work was the first I had seen which attempted to write down English in a Welsh accent.

The main difficulty in writing dialect poetry is deciding on the most accurate of the many ways words and phrases can be represented—I am still altering pieces I wrote over thirty years ago. Many readers struggle with the unorthodox spelling used. One of the rewards however is when people do connect with this 'different' language. An underlying problem with dialect writing is that it is often viewed as being inherently amusing. Some of the turns of phrase that are used in dialect are creative and can be very funny but I feel strongly that dialect poetry should not be confined to 'humorous' verse.

I would argue that dialect poetry is both parochial and universal—parochial inasmuch as it represents a specific area but universal because it deals with the emotions and issues that preoccupy all poets. It is universal because it contributes to an appreciation of different cultures and communities. Robert Frost described poetry as a way of remembering things which would otherwise be lost. Over and above what is being written about, writing in dialect is a way of recording and remembering.

Bigan Brave

See im?
Im oo jes passed.
E doan look much now
buttee woz an ero t me wen I wozzer kid
annee played futher Swans.

At woziny ole days
bfore sweepers an midfield schemers.
E wozzer Centre Forward.
Bigan brave e woz
an local too.
My ole man sawim play futher Schoolboys,
sed e addit then.

E scored goals ew thought ew couldoney dream bout.
E couldn arf giver baller welt.
Good withiz ed azwell,
eed dive in wetha boots woz flyin;
ewed think eed killizelf.
E gotter fair few bumps mine
buttee olliz cum back.
Bigan brave e woz.

Wenter playfer some English club
buttee never reely settled.
Adder bad break to iz ankle
annee woz never right after.

Somewun tole me eeze alcolic.
I knowee been drinkin evvy
ew oney gottoo look atim.

O buttee could play!
Wenny adther ball
woz lker lectric current threwer crowd.

Wunoviz goals woz like findin a fiver wenew skint.
E maydew feel good:
maydew bleevin miracles.
Awlus kids wanted t be like im.
Bigan brave.

I knoweeze in elluver state—
an doh gemmy wrong—
I'm sorry futher paw bastud,
but inner way it dunt matter woteeze like now
coz ats not owile rememberim.

Prof

E woz clever so Terry called im Prof.
Eed talkbout anythin overra pint.
Knew allsorts bout politics annat stuff,
spentages chopsin, splainin wotty meant.
Workimself uppywood an starter shout
butty didn mean no arm, an slongzy
kep to a cupla sherbets eed be orrite.
Butten e vanished frommer pub—from Swonzee.
Terry tole me later eed lossiz flat
cozzeed started drinkin evvy. Ad to sleep
onner beach — anninawinter, ass nogreat.
E woz drinkin at wite cider, roughen cheap.
Someone founim drownded arfra storm.

Prof woz orrite—e never meant no arm.

On My Life

Woz orrite a first,
I spoze I loved im.
I didn care bout iz mam
anner face liker smacked arse evrytime I called.

My mamndad wurnt too appy nyther mind,
buhwen I cort fer Laura
ay letus live withum.
My ole man annim woz olliz rowin
coz e woz goin out awler time
wile I woz getting liker bloon.
E woz even onner pisser night she woz born.

Godder place vrone yur later,
after mam wen downy ousing.
an I woz carryin Billy.
At woz wenny reely started to witme
—eed clouted me wunsor twice like—
buthis woz diffrunt.
Leasty didn kick my belly.
Never wen up mams tiller bruises went.

I didn know nowun onny sate we moved to
burree gottoo know lots downer pub,
mustuv—e woz air evry cowinight.
I didn care bout me slongzy didn toucher kids,
I wen downer welfare frelp
annay sen me some posh woman
oo talked to me like she wozzer teacher.
She did nav a clew.
Billy's cloze woz stinkin from playin outer back
an I sawer lookatim
'Do you always let your little boy get so dirty?' she said.
Stuck up bitch.

Corse e it Billy didnee?
Annee wozneven drunk.
I tole im fee did at agen I'd kilim.
On my life.
Carn member much after e gotter holt uv myair
an punched me.
Burrile never go back twim
anneel neveravver kids.
On my life.

Like Rome, like

I yurd some clever sod sed Swonzee woz like Rome,
cozzitsbilt on sevenills.

Well I've been countinumuplike.

Firstoff airze Townill
weara wether'solwez diffrunt.
Enairze Mayill rouner side annifew carryon
ew getster Greenill;
Green cozzov awlee Irish oo cum there yurzago
(wellats wot my ole man reckns anyway).

Ravenill's onnaway t Blineymice
but I never seen no ravens up air—
few jackdaws an magpies bunno ravens.
Rose ill's up be ined Uplands
ware airza quarry up by Terrace Road.
From airsclose to Constitution ill—
now that's the sort of ill ew wooden wanter climb drunk or sober.
Annover eastside airze Kilvey ill
wot everyone goze roun wennay carn tellew somethin straight.

Ats sevenills awright,
butten airza Welsh ones
coz Bryn means ill ansoduz Pen—
Brynuvrid an Brynmill, Penviliaran Penlan.
Annen Mount Pleasant's gottoo be a ill wither name lycat .
Ass twelve ann I bet I missed some.

At feller mighterbeen good at jography
Butty cooden cowin count.

Livin

Ay cawlitter sail bridge
burrit look sliker knife orra feather to me.
Makes me thinker cutting through, oflyin.

Urail is smooth ancole onnew ands
an wennew clymover ew onnew own.
Vreone else goes betweener rails
annairze me ouside, goin ware I wannoo go.

I seen pitchers oviss bit ovveriver
foray putter barrage and em yots.
Innyole days, wenner tide was out
ew cd see bitsvole boats stuck inner mud
annay jess like bones pokin up.
All covered up now,
no buggerullever see um again.
Makes me feel funny
sometimes I thinkile gecaught on one vozebones
an I gescared.

I stan ryetonny edge
anner good citin feelin anner scary feelin
gess mixed up im my chest.

Annen I feel I minner bloon orrer bubble
anawl I cunyurz my art thumpin
lykit wozzan ammer.

Annen I jess step out,
Outovver bubble
an interyair.

I doan countnor nuthin
slike my body knowzitser time
an I jess step interyair.
Slike ew know summonle be air t catchew,
atewle be safe.

Annits slow an speeded upatter sametime.
I moutovver bubble
annoises iz rushin threwmy ed
an I sees people onny other bridge pointin—
annairze me inny air
annime fallin, annime flyin.
I'm one ovoze big gulls slidin downer sky.
I'mer divin bird.

Annen I yitter water,
oney snolike water
cozzits ard bubreaks easy.
It shakes ew bones,
slaps ew about,
stings ew skin.

I seener filmovver bullet in slow motion goin through glass,
ann I thinkimer bullet
annits me breakinner glass
annairze splosions awl roun me
like bitser glass flyin everyware.
Annen I munder.
I'm shootin down, down.
Airza rushin an roarin im my ead,

like someone turned both taps full on im myurrs,
sorl churnin an bubblin.

Anenner taps aroff.
anairze no more soun.

I nevererd quiet lykit,
slike I've landed inner boxer cotton wool.
At momen doan lars long
butiss wunnover bess bits.
No wun cn gemme yur.
I'm locked up inner water but I'm free.
No souns—
silence.
Like bein buried.
Praps its lykiss wennew dead.

Burrime nodead
Cozzime so cole my ballsisin my yurs
annis lykime inner freezer
annevry bitter me stars t go lykice.

Water's nolike water now.
Sthick, liker cotton wool is squashin
grabbin my chest
squeezin my lungs tighterntighter.

I'm nothinkin bouter cole now
coz I carn breathe annive got no breath left,
so I kick an kick.
I feel Imovin up but I carn maykit.
I'm fightin,
part of me trynter force my mouth open
anny other clampin my teethen lips tgether.
I burst outerer water liker bullet comin back
anmy lungsiz on fire
an I dunno fy should breathe innorout
annime choking n laughin at the same time.

Iffy other bitslike dyin
issiz like bein born.
Babies do come out sudden
inner squirtin wet rush.
An I feel great
lykime new annat was my first breath ever.

An I know I gottoo do it gain
Eveno evrytime I do it I'm scared shitless.

Butairze things ew knowew jess gotter do—
cozzits livin.

Jess like ewan me

Issis bousfar as I cn manage now.
Empty crispacket olds more airn my lungs.
Airs ewjly a bench I can sit on.
I cannavva look atta river an awlem new bildins.
I cn ardly member ware things ewsed t be.
Someone inny ome sedday built otels n things jess byer Princer Wales dock.
Ooder thought it!
Ewseter livin Sain Thomas.
From owrouse ew cd see a railway sidins.
anner trucks beein shunted rouna docks.
Anna big boats—awler freighters, trawlers n tankers comin in an out byer pier.
Ay come from allover a world t Swonzee.

I yurd somewunnonner telly say time's liker river.
Well ayve sopped a clock onnis one withat barrage—or lease made it go reel slow.
Didn avter walk tooer beach to knowa tides before.
The sea come right into a river, creepin upper banks
annen wenna tide turned, arriver shrunk ry down
annit was likittle stream inner mud.
Annew cd smeller mud—a ronk like nuthin else.
Cd smell all sorts innit—sea anny earth an dead things and live things all mixed up.

Wennwe woz kids meenmy sisters ewseter go tooer Gospel Awl
annay ewsed to get us t singer song bout bein washed inner river
an wile I woz croakin away I was thinkin
bouter Towee. Awl oily n muddy.
I thought iffay washed me there, I'd be dirtier comin out than I was goin in.
Yea — it mattud t me t see the river movin wither tide.
Carn see nuthin no more not evena mud.

My ole man come downter Swonzee
wenny woz fifteen from upper varley—
proppa Welsh e woz.
Ewseter sing twuss kids in Welsh. I cn still member bits ovoze ole songs,
but God knows wottay mean, cozzy never tole us.
E seddy come down coz e didden wannoo work inner mine—
said iz father go kilt wenner roof give in.
Tole iz mam e woz goin t Swonzee t be a sailor. E never did though.
Owney sailin e ever did woz onner Campbell steamer t Ilfracombe.
E woz sick azzer dog aller way air anawler way back.
Funny thing though—e ended up shovelin coal.
E become a coal trimmer downer docks.

I like iss fancy bridge ayve put up by yur.
Loss of people onnitterday.
See at couple bein awl lovey-dovey, cwtshin up close t look down atter water?
Meenmy Betty ewsed t do at—owney at was onny ole bridge.
Ats ware we gorringaged.
Burrit awl started wither big row. Carn reely member wotit woz bout.
Probly me goin wither boys onner Satday night
wennit woz sposed t be ower night out.
Anyway we woz walkin overa bridge avven our row
wen allova sudden Betty runs off—reel angry an takes offa ring I give er.
It wasn posh nor nuthin—I foun it onner beach.
But I knew it meant a lot to Betty.
She was tampin now an I thought she was goin t throw it inner river.
She ad ellova tempa mine did Betty.
She eld at ole ring up an I felt my art turn over.
Betty meant a lotter me. Trouble was I wasn very good at sayin it.

But she sawer look on my face an she knew I did care.
She eld a ring overer side ovver bridge an sed
'Wossit t be then Tommy Jenkins? Eithera ring goes inner river or it goes yur.'
An she puts it on top ov er weddin finger.
Well—at woz it.
An I knew it was right.

She been gone a long time now, Betty. An I do misser still.
Ats wy I like comin down yur.
It wozzer special place fruss.

She never saw iss new bridge.
She woulduv liked it.
Woulduv seen at couple with they eds tgether lookin atteriver.
An I cn yurrer say
'Jess like ewan me Tommy. Jess like ewan me.'

Fewnruls

I domine goanter fewnruls.
Ay sad orrite, buttew gotter go—
show ew respecks.

Mosser upper crem.
Airze nomuch room upair.
If airzer big crowd
ew knows someone's gone before ayer time
but if airzeplentya seats it's some poor bugger
ooze lived longerun awliz famlyeen frens.
I olliz gofits anole mate from work
orfits someone frommer street.
Ileven gofitsomeone I doan like—
gottoo show ew respecks.

The singin in the crem's awl gone a bit arf arted
speshly iffay singin ims.
No one knowser words no more.
Wunsor twice I beenter fewnruls inner church or chapel.
Awler reglars knows outer beyave.
Urrestuvus avter watchum, with awler bobbin uppendown.
Butter singin's better.
Sumvoze Welsh ims can makew back go awl prickly.

Oze vicars go on bout lifafter death
Noshewer bout at.
Butter portant thingster be there
forrer frens an family—
show ew respecks.

I doan like avinter speaktuer usband or wife
or oo evers left.
I carn say awloze soothing words but I join a queue
An wennis my turn I say sumthin
Evenifs jess 'Sorry for ew trouble.'

No, domine fewnruls,
But I noticed larse time upper crem
I'm getting much closer twer front seats.

Stephen Knight

The poems are in a phonetic Swansea accent, so it helps to read them aloud (or hear me read them with a copy of the poems to hand!). The first was written in 1986, when I had been away from Swansea for a few months. Sitting on the back of a bus on the way to my parents' home, I could hear a couple of girls chatting at the front. I couldn't make out what they were saying, but I could hear the particular sounds of the accent: the pronunciations, the rhythms, the intonations.

I had missed those sounds (accent is place), so I wanted to capture them in poems. They are the invented, challenging-to-decipher tongue of a monoglot with an Austrian mother who nevertheless feels Welsh. What was said in the poems was less important to me than how it was said—to assert that this voice has value, too—though it was impossible not to depict in the process a city and a people reduced by successive Tory Governments. Written in the late 1980s/early 1990s, the first attempts are dramatic monologues. When I revisited the style just under ten years ago, the results were autobiographical. They might be even more tricky to 'translate.' By then, I had lived away for more years than I had lived in Wales.

At the Foot of Division Four

Ow footbawlTeem wares blackenwhite:
a angz a reds, a looks kuntrite
fuhlOozin, Homer N'weigh,
buhstill aisle go unwatchum-play
in Winter wenner Windsor blowin
9gaylz offaSee unthrowin
rubbish rowndee airmTee stanz,
blowin ice throo my airmTee ands.

John Toshack wozzer-marrNidjer-wenn
a roe-zupp 2 Division won.
Enner sighed wasFuller codjers
attee-endov Ayr Koreas;
e boreTum fuhPeenutz neigh played
foruh season. Nunnervumstaid,
uh-gnat wozzer long thymer go.
Now we backin Division Phaw!

Prap zitzer clymitt aura food
innease parts duzzEwe so muchgood
eye-dun-owe, buttie oldest laydee
inner Brittish Aisles livzbuymee,
inner Gnome. Givorrtayker year
ov breethin Saul tea Swornzee Heir
sheezer nundruden-nighn, unTV
filmzer birthdaze rare gullully.

Sheezlimp, tie-udd, uvairj Tubble:
ur riser bearLeigh vizzible
re-seedin inner-red: ur skinz
udared, crakt Riverbared nuthinz
swammerbuv frayJiz: wenner voyss
leex throo gapZinnerShrungkunFayce
shee sairz sodAwl turimEmber
(lyke pose cards senTinDissember,

nuthin air Butter Sea nurry).
Air vreethin z'owld innis cuntree—
gray ills, gray trees Anna poe-stuh
s'been stuckon Neath stayshun frair-vuh:
iss flew-rare-sunt unrareLidjuss
wither quaresChunn inbiggLairtuzz,
aniss quaresChunn tare-riff-eyes me.
Where will YOU spend Eternity?

(1987)

The Heart of Saturday Night

IssFair wuz-honourCaw-munlarzSatdee:
doorjums, toff yapples, goalfish. Lie kytowld,
wee wenhonourGhosetrayn, mean Bare vully.-

z'krap. Unwenchy wear gnome twavver-tee,
try duhWallsuz. Brill! Addter-reely old.
IssFair wuz-honourCaw-munlarzSatdee.

Ease werkinnerWallsuz awlnite wunny,
issgeezerKev eyesoreAir. Ease reel ye'owld.
Wee wenhonourGhosetrayn, mean Bare vully.

WenairwuzzerwindblowinoffaSee
izzreelyNoblin... Jeezus, *coarse* eyezcold—
IssFair wuz-honourCaw-munlarzSatdee,

caw-munzfuhkinfree zin!... Ease twennyfree,
Kev: why tandzAnna chaynmaydoubter-gold.
Wee wenhonourGhosetrayn, mean Bare vully.

Kev addSmak (whytes tough) asswaddyshowdme
Om-eye-life! Sed easegonergerrit souled.
IssFair wuz-honourCaw-munlarzSatdee.
Wee wenhonourGhosetrayn, mean Bare vully.

Port Talbot

AirzeeM4 runinonnyEdger-town.
Kahzgo-zbuy awlerThyme brissplay scissor-sairntunce

withOwtennyverrb—sunobbsuleetnown!
Signs in Well shunning Lish, Sundaze go-nonfer munce.

See kumzgray upperbeach; kidzgoZinnerwayvz
unkem-culls goZonum. Rhodezizgray undirty

butt Yew/nyun Jarx—payntid, reign-warsht—payvz
ease payvmuntz. Bee nare sincerQween'z Jew Billy.

Sceptre-lites frommerWhirxx, sungoZnit Saul Black
ne'er zustink, unsmowk unlitesLyke DIE-MUNZ awe-wytes

uvize, lyke warter honour shy-kneeMac,
spar klinlyker notion: yare lowlites unwyte lites

unflaymz eye honour stax burnin gas
2eye L. Burnininner darkness.

A Swansea Adolescence

Aye, one dud: lone Leigh . . .

Fairs 'whirreds' a tome
  eye Aster Rome—
s'coal dazzer Sore Bay
  in cider nowt.
  So, Kaye

skull kzinner lie
  brie crip Linley shy
Anna lie No sk'wee
  kz'lie cunNinj.
  Bowie m'yun me,

eye-make snow sound
  sigh dull-inner round:
my *fleadh* pin-flares,
  my dare zutBoots—
  sh—honour stares.

TEAR S'AIR L'YUT
  TEAR NISSEN
RAW JUMMER GOFF
  TEAR DUES unSHAY
  MACINI

Honour bee chore-
  vunny vning, spore
t'zungry sea lox—a ne'er
  fin pane! Bry
  dunk air

zlong as eyes outside
  Waugh chinner tied—
sh—bray kinner part
  honour Shaw, unPhil
  in my art

air gnome trite
  Bard vur Saul Night
oo nose wof-Phaw—
  eye done
  no maw.

In This Dream of Swansea

eye m'honour-bussOhm

inner paw rinn-reign

nigh muddlinin Shah doze

Anna dry vrizDard

an we go in a pill

a knees way vinnizand

is in Dick ate inand

N we tern ínfer Rome

dhow nils an a pills

inner dry Vin reign

nigh no ease m'eyed 'ard

eave no easin' Shah doe

a gnaw Ribble Shah doze

‘ullo din my ands

un bear re: Ind ‘ard

a ne’er Naim a tome

O minner reign

enow ow! s’*honi* ill

honi eye ist ill

nis coal dun airs Shah doze

a ne’ers bucker tin Raine

a nigh olds out my ands

a nigh Sir Chiz my ohm

Sir Chin Fudd ‘ard

Sir Chin Fudd ‘ard

enow ow! s’*honi* ill

Sir Chiz ow! Rome

she tiddin Shah doze

to old is and

one s'maw inner reign

inner gore doorful reign

nigh'm bare low inDARD

a zigh olds owt my and

enow ow! s'*honi* ill

re: chinnin Shah doze

re: chin bar comb

Anna Raine runs a pill

undar dizzer Shah Doe

innis dreamer v'Ohm

Brian Phillips

I was born in Llansamlet, Swansea, which in 1956 still bore the scars of WW2. That, and deindustrialization and decline, had bequeathed to me a toxic, "lunar", wasteland, as my playground. The decline began well before Thatcher applied the 'coup de grace', but not before the decay and gloom of the place, along with the toxins in the soil, had seeped into my subconscious and into my bones, to surface, years later, in the pain of my writing. Few things inspire me more than being miserable, nostalgic and righteously embittered by an irredeemable past.

My Dad, Tom Kingsley, spoke English with a deep Swansea accent and 'particular' syntax, bordering on dialect. My mother was English, so Dad reined-in his first language, Cymraeg. He kept it as a private language for old friends and family when things of dire import, eg: the "bithin-gallew-ahn-wod-avew", were discussed around me. Thus 'Cymraeg' became an exotic mystery to me, despite my living in the faltering industrial heart of 'Cymru'.

I had all the Swansea characteristics of speech by 1962, when, on my 6th birthday, we moved to Luton, where I discovered that I didn't speak English in any fathomable form, nor did anyone else there. I "localised" within months, and my "Wodd-ew-torkin-bough-now-mun?" became "Wochoo-on-abah'-nah-ma'e?"

In 1966 we moved back to Swansea. Again, no-one spoke my 'English', and to avoid daily violence, I re-acquired the local lingo. No wonder I find variances within a language so fascinating. Though most of my poetry is not in dialect or accent, I love the 'mechanics' of capturing genuine voices, despite the difficulties.

Five phenomenal writers inspired me to try expressing dialect in my poetry. They are: Russell Hoban; whose masterpiece, *Riddley Walker*, opened my eyes to the beauty of language evolution; Flann O'Brien; whose book *An Béal Bocht* (*The Poor Mouth*) wrapped its rain-sodden, hilarious language around my heart and never let go; Stephen Knight; another 'Swansea Jack', whose revelatory *A Swansea Love Song* shows our own 'language' to us in a completely new way; Mike Jenkins; who writes dialect more fluently and observantly than anyone I know, and whose book *From Aberfan t Grenfell* haunts your head with the genuine voices of the Valleys; and the late Nigel Jenkins, whose outrageously unrestrained poem 'The Language of Love' says so much about Swansea's use or abuse of English in so few words.

Them vs Us

We ghesson very nicely
tilla derby comes aroun.
Then it's "Bastad Jack or FfukinTaff,
few goes up, ewll be back down."

Now, one thing's always bothered me,
Iss childish an absurd,
Tha both teams ave a 'nick-name'
thas juss a pretty bird.

Imagine, right beforah game,
ew tries to give ewah team some hwyl
Up the Swans or Come on Bluebirds
would take they-uh passion offa boil.

We noh Will ah Bard, nor Vera Lynne,
We noh from Stratford nor from Dover.
Would ew call a rabid Bulldog "Fluffy"?
We needs to thinkiss name thing over.

The name should rouse, in others, dread,
An make uh visitin teams afraid,
An let 'em know they'll soon be dead,
orra least in need of some first aid.

The Swans could be The Vikings
'cause Swansea was Sweyn's Ey,
The Bluebirds more like Seagulls,
oo rob ewah chips azay go by.

Owahr National game as diffran rools,
wheruh noise turns visitors' blood to ice,
aan one rule stands above 'em all,
"At all costs, beattah bloody Saes".

We lovezee Irish, loves uh Scots,
Italians are all owah mates,
We respectsuh bloody French a lot,
Iss juss-uh bloody Saes we ates!

When tha day comes roun once a yur,
With joy an rapture unsurpassed,
We sheds a patriotic tear
An watchuh Saes get far outclassed,

And even if we loosuh game
there's one thing tharrey wonebee winnin.
Iddenns up every time uh same.
We'll thrashah Saes at bloody singin.

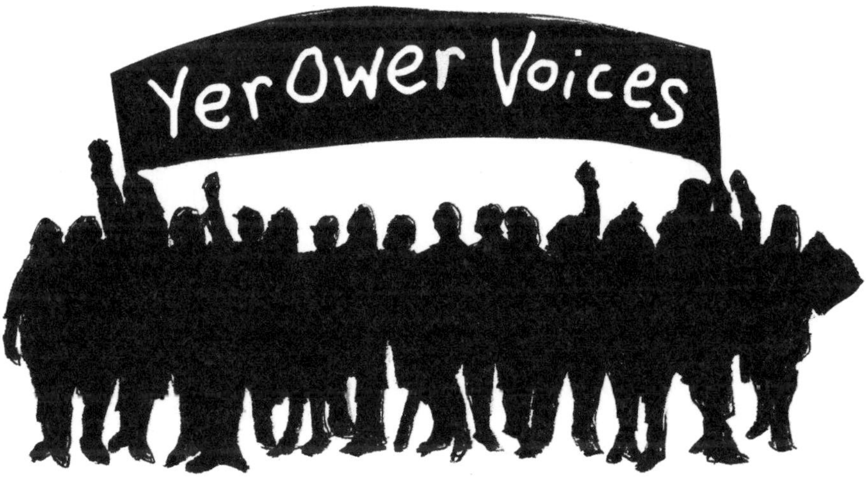

Anne Phillips

I am Swansea born and bred, with an MA in Creative Writing in Context from Bangor University. I lived in Ynys Môn and worked as a teacher and lecturer of English in Coleg Menai, Bangor and schools in Gwynedd and Ynys Môn. Matt Smith (Black Bough Poetry) is my mentor.

Accent and dialect are signifiers of home, they can also be sources of gentle amusement, affectionate teasing and occasionally contempt. They can also indicate that a person is an outsider when the dialect is unfamiliar: *cwni lan, cwyd fyny, coda lan* all mean get up in Swansea Valley, North Wales and West Wales, respectively. *Parcods* (chicks) are *cywion bach* depending on where you live; and in pockets of Gwynedd, *Cer mas* was a foreign language; a source of confusion, hilarity and on one occasion anger because the person I was addressing had no idea what I meant. One thing is clear though. A Swansea accent caused *hiraeth*: I longed for family and home even though they no longer existed.

My influences are the voices I hear daily in the city when I'm working: fruit and flower vendors, coffee shops, cockle stalls and butchers' shops in Swansea market. The accent signifies home, a place where I feel I belong—the place where I feel more myself than anywhere else. It's the accent of a city where I collide with younger versions of myself: the one who couldn't wait to leave and the one who couldn't wait to return.

I now live in Swansea and work for a charity which supports carers from 16 to 102. I work specifically with young adult carers aged 16 to 25. I write in dialect because it is the sound of my home town and the way my parents and grand-parents spoke. Someone a long time ago told me that they worked hard to lose their accent as if it were a source of shame. I write in dialect because it's possible to explore universal themes and firmly locate them in a geographical place.

The main challenge of writing in dialect is that it could be seen as making fun of a regional accent, diminishing the person or subject. I hope this is a sympathetic poem about the real challenges that face carers and families throughout Wales.

True Story Dementia Hub, Christmas 2022

I ony popd in like,
Wanted iw to know.
Is sbin evah so saad,
an ees rili baad,
ees nor the same man.
No' cocker the walk
ees jus gone—
shrunk away—over the
laas three four weeks.
Lookin baad ee is now
like out of it
an nuthin much there
ees nor with us much—
iss bin evah so quick
forgettin to eat and forgettin to drink
ees bin so proud and strong
iss nor my dad eny more
zif ee no longer with us.
I jus can' stop cryin—
an iss Christmas an all!
Look ar the state on me!
I'll be ol rite
Merry Christmas an thanks
Thanks evah so much
Sgonna be 'ard but we'll get there
Gonna miss im so much!

Wha Yew On-Nah Bout?

—The Valleys

Gemma June Howell

I've been writing and performing South Walian valleys dialect poetry for over ten years, and people always say that it's much better when they hear me read it rather than when it is written. To most, I just write funny poems from the perspective of the people society forgot. Some might say that dialect poetry is inaccessible, but I believe that it is quite the opposite: dialect poetry provides a valuable gateway into other cultures and communities and is ultimately a reclamation of cultural identity, through voice.

I've also been an English teacher for ten years. I've taught poetry and with *any* poem, you have to read it several times to understand it. So, when people say that dialect poetry is not accessible in its written form, that isn't the case at all. Just because someone can't instantly recognise the syntax, they write it off. But, what they're actually doing is writing off the voice from where it comes. Poetry isn't just about using clever literary devices and superfluous language, it is about getting to the heart of what it means to be alive and reflecting who we are in the context of the universality of the human condition.

My first encounter with dialect poetry was with the Red Poets. I was only 16 at the time, and my grandmother, who was a community councillor, introduced me to Tim Richards who's a journalist, poet and represented the Bedwas miners during the 1980s strikes. I remember having a moment of clarity when I first read his poem, 'Back to Basics Crap': a snapshot of the life of a single mother living on a council estate in the Thatcher era. Having lived on Graig-Y-Rhacca, in the South Wales valleys, I was part of the life he portrayed; however, I had not heard anyone defending or fighting back using the written word in the voices of those actually living that life.

At my first Red Poets night, I remember buying a small pamphlet, which I still go back to today, and in this pamphlet, I read Jazz's 'Giro City', and Penny Windsor's 'Crashing the Moon'—and despite being written in standard English, the poems gave me the impetus to write what I saw, what we lived in our words. Within the pamphlet, edited by Mike Jenkins, I also read 'Big Mick', which was the first time I'd ever come across dialect poetry. However, I didn't actually write my first dialect poem until I started the MA in Creative Writing at Swansea university. It was the late Nigel Jenkins who interviewed me, then championed my vernacular stuff. He told me to go further and encouraged me to read the excellent dialect works of Scottish poets, Don Paterson and James Kelman.

So, "further" I went—but not so much in terms of phonetics, which has developed over time, but more so in subject matter. I'd already read Irvine Welsh's *Acid House* and *Trainspotting*, which despite being set in Scotland, I knew his characters; I'd grown up with them. In my first book, *Inside the Treacle Well*, I drew inspiration from the darkest and riskiest places and experimented with the vernacular of my home town.

When I discovered Benjamin Zephaniah, I fell in love with how he expressed patois on the page. I grew up surrounded by '80s reggae and ska; Bob Marley, Tracey Chapman, UB40, and later, hip-hop artists, Salt 'n' Pepper and Tupac Shakur, whose life experiences resonated strongly with my own and those I loved, lived and battled alongside. On the estate, the street was our stage, and I think that it was these early influences that shaped the way I write and express myself.

Over the years my work has won some people over, inspiring some people from Graig-Y-Rhacca in their own artistic endeavours, but it's also received much condemnation with audience members heckling or flat-out walking out, and organisers apologising for my words. This way of writing has not always been accepted on the page, but as Benjamin Zephaniah said: 'Dis poetry is not afraid of going ina book / Still dis poetry need ears fe hear an eyes fe hav a look.'

For me, dialect writing is what it is: unashamedly *real*. To my knowledge, there's only a handful of dialect poets in Wales who are chartering new ground. Over time, I've developed my own phonetics which are specific to the Rhymney valley, however I often read the way Mike Jenkins spells some words, and I think—*damn, that sounds much better, why didn't I think of saying it like that?*

But despite our differences and nuances of phonetic selection, I think that we are all trying to achieve the same goal and that is to invite the reader or audience into unknown worlds—worlds that are often misrepresented, stigmatised or maligned. We shed some light on the vibrancy of these forgotten communities, inviting readers and audiences to hear the voices of those who inhabit those worlds in all their unique glory.

Normull

Ee wuz a'right when
I firss met 'im.
Reallee ee wuz.
Reallee charmen un tha'.
        Nice like.
Tuk me out un stuff.
Fuh meals un tha'.
It wuz nice like.
It wuz normull.

Aftah th'bairbee cum-oh,
ee've changed.
Eez nastee now.
Cums in pist un tha'.
Smashez up ee 'ouse.

My muv-vah tells me tuh
"stick it out"
An' my fartha likes im too,
cuz *"ee duz his duty"*
an tha's gud enuff fuh rim.

Aftah the bairbee cum
ee started puttin' ci-duh
in my yer evree mornin.
Ee tapes it up
an if I take it off
ee gives me a slap.

I nevuh tole m'muthuh
abou' tha' mind.
She'd gor mad mun.
She likes 'im see
cuz eez nice when
she cums round

t'pick up th'Bairbee.
 Aftah th'bairbee cum, ee
started checkin the 'ouse.
Checkin t'see if iss clean.
Eee saw sum serial killah
oo did it onuh tellee
Eez eevun got white gloves
un evreefin.

An' now eev started checkin mee wiv um too.

Dirty Pill

Cun ewe still remembuh
when we ewst tuh play
roun' by th'fishshop
and in by the flats
ev-ree fucken day?

Smorken' marawarnah
nuffin elss tuh doo.
Alwez on the lookout
fuh somefin fucken' new.

Cun ewe still remembuh
nights on Valium.
Tamarzies or Diarzies
tha' yew pinched off yuh mum.

Neckin um wi'vodka
un' spewin up our guts.
Lyin on the football pitch,
off our fucken nuts.

Cun ewe still remembuh
picken Magies up uh field.
Eatin um up there and then,
laffin till we peed.

Cun ewe still remembuh
sittin on tha' crate?
Blockin out the cold,
downin vodka straight.

Cun ewe still remembuh
tha' night on dirty Pukkuz.
Yeah, we were propa off it butt
dodgy lickle fukkuz.

We wuh in-uh club in Kah-diff,
slammin' uh dance-floor.
They torld us to stop butt,
I wish we 'ad no more.

A Social Call

Tha' stuck up bitch,
oo th' fuck does shee
think shee iz?

Cumin' in yuh,
norsing about.
Tryin tuh find someink wrong
wi'my kids.

Drugs?!
Where th' fuck did she ge' tha' frum?
Thar norzee cow nex' door,

alwez watchin' or-vuh thuh fence,
askin if th' kidz uh a'right.

My fuckin kidz uh fine mun!
Juss leave us alorn.
If I couldunt look aftuh um
I wudent uv fuckin ad um
would I?

I meen wha's she cumin yer for?
Tha' bitch orvuh thuh way leaves 'er kids
in thuh garden when she goes fuh ruh pint.
I seen um cwtched up in thuh coal shed wiv the dogs.
Why izunt shee orvuh there instead?

They juss dunt like us
cuz we're an 'ard family.
Singulling us out cuz we go' uh
repu-tair-shun.
My kids are juss uz good uz
enee-wun else's.
I meen,
where's 'er qualificair-shuns?
Sheez on-uh fuckin place-munt
fuh Coh-lidge.
A'right fuh sum mind.
Avunt evun got kidz of 'er own.
Sheez no' frum yere.
If shee did, sheed knaw ow bludee 'ard it is espe-shully up yere.

Dun eevun knaw wha's sheez taking uh-bout.
Shee avunt go' a fuckin clue.
I'mah gud muvva.
Doo my best cunsiduh-rin.

Benefit Fraud

Wha yew on-nah bout, fraud?
No ifs, nor buts?
What th' fuck!
I aven dun nuffin!
Onest I avunt.
Yew bastads owe me
twoo fucken weeks.
Yewah the fucken
fraudsters Butt, no' me.
I go' nor wun livin yuh.
Juss me un m'nippa like.

Wha' yew gunna do?
Stop my mun-nee
cuz sum ole bitch told yew
I ad a womun yuh?
Aye, my siss-tuh!
She bairbee-sits ev'ree Fursday like.
I told ewe iss buh'fore.
Check yewer cum-poo-tah.
Wha, yew gunna stop m' munee
cuz uv tha'like?
Bollucks!
Yew alred-dee tuk
fiftee quid off my 'ousin.

Crisis lorn?
I paid it all off mun!
I go' thuh lettah somewhere.
Hang on....
Bollocks like!
I'll gor tuh yewer fucken boss then,
see wha ee sez.
She?
No wunda yew carn doo yuh job en.

Workin?
I aven worked since nine-teen ninetee three,
When 'ey closed down thuh factree.
No jobs round yuh Butt.
—Yew should know thah mun.

I live in the Valley's, ooz gunna employ me?
Get on-nuh bike tuh Cardiff?
Yew fink bikes, buses, trains uh free?

Oh Butt, juss lissun tuh meee.
I'm no' thuh wun ooz feevin yuh,
iss the Guv-uh-munt see.

Yewuh the fucken fraudstuz butt, no' mee.

Yew owe me butt!
I need tha' fucken mun-nee.

Another Bun in the Oven

A'rite? Nairmz Rhiannon,
an I leve on thuh Rock.
I luv drinken ciduh,
an I luv sucken cock.

I wanna bee yin college,
buh I go' uh lickle kid.
An-uh crèche in college
aint tha fucken big.

My muvva wun elp me,
cuz I nict er tellee.
An my ole man iza preck.
Ee puncht er in th'bellee.

Nutz in skool, I wuz.
Chucken chairz un sellen fagz.
Expelled ut firteen, I wuz,
f'robbin uh teachuz bagz.

It wuz f'thuh best ough,
I wuz pregnunt wiv Levi,
Mist all uv my examz, I ded.
Tuh my life I sed g'bye.

My felluz shaggen round,
iss bin gor en ona wi-yul.
Iss bairbeez bout t'drop soon.
Weyull gor on Jeremee ki-yul.

Sor, I angah round uh shops,
tuh see oo eez shaggen.
All-uh boyz cum on tuh me,
finken *I'm* out slaggen!

My boobs uh fucken killin
An my belleez rock ard.
Bastad duzunt giva shit,
now eez wiv iz new tart.

Anuva kid.
Anuva Giro.
Iz tha all wee-yuh werff?
Iz ent air more too wis yere life
un givin fuckin berff?

Anuva drink.
Anuva fag.
Anuva spliff,
or pill.

Wee-yuh fucken ewmuns yuh,
not pigs in fucken swill!

Jobseeker's Disagreement

Slept in past twelve again tuh-day,
thuh Bair-leffs woke mee yup.
There's nor milk in thuh fridge again
an I carn find uh clean cup.

Stuck in iss coun-sull flat all day,
gettin smashed wiv friends.
Avunt go' thuh munee fuh fags
so we make doo wiv dog-ends.

Thuh fack-tree where we ewest tuh work
closed down wiv nor forewarnin.
They moved to China, way back now,
when new industry wuz dawnin.

So, on nah New Deal course I went,
tuh polish up some skills.
Aftuh tha' I wuz on th'sick,
uddicted to 'appy pillz.

Stuck in iss coun-sull flat all day,
shuvell-lin beans on toar-st.
Watchin Jeremy Ki-yul repeats,
could murder a Sunday roar-st!

Applied fuh ruh bar job in Spoons,
searched fuh work on thuh net.
Applied uz un office monkey,
but nuffin uz cum up yet.

I typed up uh ree-sunt C.V.
Blitzed it like confetti.
If nor wun wanss my ser-vi-siz,
I'll burn my fuckin settee!

Wen' tuh sign on larss Fursday again.
Go' sank-shuned on my munee. They say:
"You broke the Jobseeker's Agreement...
Checked job seck-shun Tuesday 'stead of Monday."

Sor obviously I wuz tampin.
All I said wuz "this is wank."
Now I'm fuckin banned frum there
an livin off thuh food bank.

Head Hunted

Wha' yew doo-in sittin exams?
Yew carn av thah where
wee-yuh frum.

See 'em by there?
—Pushin prams.
Tha's where yew-uh frum.

Sor wha' thuh fuck ewe doo-in?
Suckin thuh teachuz arse,
Iss yew their fuckin screwin.
Yew-will nevuh fuckin pass.

Cum-un work fuh me.
I swear yew'll make a bomb.
If ewe dun't say yeah now
the off-fuh will bee gone.

The nipperz oo 'ang round us
Avunt gotta clue.
Cum-mon mun, join me Butt.
Ansuz up tuh yew.
Cum-mon mun, sellin iz-ah skill

an' I need sum-wun like ewe
tuh pump thuh fuckin pills.
I go' no-wun down thuh skoo-ul
an yew knaw I'm banned
frum there.
Will ewe doo it fuh mee butt?
An wha' we make,
we share.

Uni? Uni?!
Yew wanna bee-ya bum?
Yew wanna scav ow-wah tax-ez!
Yew fuckin scavin scum.

Why dun ewe wanna work fuh me?
Yew'll see thuh bucks roll in.
Iss bettuh thun bein' on thuh Dorle
an iss bettuh thun bein' skint.

Books? Books?!
Fuckin rorch material fuh yah spliff Butt.
Yew carn buy books wiv-out dollah Muckah
cuz munee makes thuh worl' gor round.
Un tha's wha' I'm off-rin Butt;
munee fuh school see...
I juss wanna 'elp ewe Butt;
tuh ge' yuh Duh-gree.

Cum-mon mun.
Dun be tight.
I need ewe down th' school,
Cum see me tuh-night.
I'll sort ewe out butt,
un tell yew wha t'do.
I need ewe Butt,
'onest Butt,
I real-lee fuckin doo.

Siôn Tomos Owen

I am a bilingual creative from the Rhondda Fawr. After experiencing over a hundred different jobs I'm now a freelance creative working as an illustrator and caricaturist, writer, presenter, and tutor with my company, CreaSion. I've published prose, poetry, comics and books for Welsh learners as well as illustrating Wales Book of the Year nominated books. I live with my wife and daughters in Treorchy, Rhondda Fawr.

I write in a Rhondda dialect, although it could be said that it is a broader Mid Glamorgan Valleys accent with some specific colloquialisms. I chose to write like this while studying Rhondda writing at university and noticed that certain stories by Gwyn Thomas, Ron Berry and Jack Jones had dialect but were tidied up, whereas *Grits* by a contemporary Welsh author Nial Griffiths was wonderfully phonetic and specific to accents.

I also enjoyed that my dialect poems, unlike my other poems, would sound unique when I performed them, rather than a jigsaw puzzle when read on the page. Some say this is a hindrance to the flow of the poem but then they've said that about the way Ida talk in real life and all. I remember hearing a comedy album called *Talk Tidy: The Art of Speaking Wenglish* by John Edwards which honed in on these South Wales Valley colloquialisms as a stand-up routine and specifically "The Ida Complex" which is related to translating English directly from Welsh. "Dwi yn" "I do", phonetically becomes "Ida", rather than the grammatically correct, "I am". "Dwi yn mynd i'r dafarn" should be the basic noun of, "I am going to the pub" but "Ida go to the pub" has a history of language to it. Another is "mun", which is used extensively in *How Green Was My Valley* but as the confusing "Man" as if the miners are all Malibu surfers.

Dialect writing is parochial which is why it speaks so well to the local, and I want to write for my people. If it's appreciated further afield then great, but shows like *The Wire* have proven that intricate parochial language can become universally appreciated when it's used well, in a way that invites intrigue in the use of language other than Standard English.

Cuppa in CA CLUD

(*After Hywel opening a cafe in his mam's kitchen when she was away*)

Kieran make one full breakfast will u?
cuppa?
ta.
thank you please
whats on ur knees
mud mun,
chelsea bun?
no ta
custard cream?
go on en, two sugars please
the man said, standin
in my mothers kitchen
i said no thanks im sweet enough
well tough, i ain't
diabetic?
no
oh
he said
hobnobs?
hobnobs i said no
oh....
crap shop this is
this ain't a shop, but, i said
it's my mothers kitchen
is it?
aye
well bugger me
no thanks im sweet enough
comical
what's the sign outside en?
what sign?
that sign by there, CA CLUD
that said CATREF CLUD

but old Trevor nicked the middle
Trev's with a V init?
i told him that but he's daft see
daft is he?
aye he's daft twice
where is he now en?
gone
oh
aye
i'll leave then shall i?
aye
hm
so long then
shall i wash the mug?
don't be soft
i'll go en
go on en
so long en
ta-ra

Kee, aws that breakfast coming?

Barry Taylor

I'm a minority within a minority within a minority: an autistic Welsh-speaking Buddhist! I'm the product of a South Wales mining community, the first generation of my family in centuries not to work underground. It could be argued that I'm actually trilingual, since I speak my native language of Wenglish alongside Welsh and English.

Wenglish, or Valleys English as it's sometimes known, is more than just another dialect of English. It is basically English vocabulary overlaid on Welsh grammar, and like all languages and dialects it has a beauty all of its own.

Regional dialects have too often been ridiculed and seen as lesser versions of a standard language, but in reality, no-one speaks standardised languages in their day-to-day life. Everyone speaks a dialect; it's just that some dialects are associated with those who have influence or political power and are thus seen as more correct by association.

I reject the nonsensical idea that any dialect can be seen as better or worse than another. Poets such as Mike Jenkins have long shown that it's possible to express the full range of human emotions and literary genres in regional dialects, and I'm conscious that I'm standing on their shoulders when I write in my own dialect.

When I write in my own dialect, some choices have to be made regarding spelling conventions. The pronunciations of Wenglish words don't always map precisely to standard English orthography, but neither does it make sense to me to use Welsh spelling conventions alongside English ones in the same piece of writing, even when they more correctly convey the pronunciation of a specific word, since not everyone is conversant with both systems.

The idiosyncratic spellings within any piece of dialect work are chosen as much for aesthetic as for practical reasons. I have chosen the spellings that I feel best match the way my dialect was spoken where I grew up; in South Wales the dialect of every valley, and even every village, is slightly different.

So why do I write in 'e way I do do it? Well, iss cuz I do talk like 'iss in real life, an I do love 'ow it do sound in 'e mouth, so I wanted to purrit on 'e page for others to enjoy an' all. Right proud o ower dilect I am, an I reckon iss about time i' wuz treated wi' a bit o respect.

Black Ole

Wen I wus young
An my dad wus still alive
'E tol me bout is days down 'e pit.
Never cared much back en,
Burr I gorrw say
'E more I do think bout it
'E less I do like 'e idea.
Packed in a cage
Aged fourteen—
Fourteen!—
Down into 'e dark,
With is art in iz mouth
As 'e cage do fall
Down a big black ole
Where ew ca'n see yooer and
In front o yooer face
an 'e ool place
Is blacker an Thatcher's art.
Bu then Thatcher come, o course
An 'e ool place
Everywhere ew looked
Felt er and orrite.
A big black ole
Where 'e ammer fell
An 'e art o the c'munity
Disappeared in 'e dark.
Nineteen-Eighty-Four,
An en 'e mines
Wus all packed up.
We din like it—all ower dads laid off.
We do try not to think bout it
Burr I gorrw say,
If ew le yooerself care,
Yooer art drops in a diff'rent dark pit.
Thank god my dad en yer no more
To fall down 'a black ole.

Phil Knight

One of my earliest memories is being taken by my Gran in the early 1970s to the Windsor Cinema in Neath to see the Dr. Who movie double bill: *Dr. Who and the Daleks* (1965) and its sequel *Daleks—Invasion 2150 A.D.* (1966).

In the movies Dr. Who is played by Peter Cushing (and yes in the film the character is actually named Dr. Who), but the Daleks are the real stars. At the time I had only seen *Doctor Who* on a small black-and-white TV. So to see the Daleks on the big screen in glorious Technicolour was mind-blowing. It was the wrong actor playing the Doctor, the TARDIS had the wrong sound effects and the music was wrong. But these Daleks were real. Real DALEKS really invading the Earth in the real, actual future. Well that's what I thought at the time, (okay I admit it I still think that, sort of). According to my Gran, I just sat there with my mouth open in shock and wonder every time the Daleks appeared on the screen.

I have been a science fiction fan ever since. But Doctor Who in all his or her forms is still my favourite. And thus I began my lifelong quest to write in Dalek. And that is why Dalek writing is so important to me, as to hear that tone of voice puts me back in contact with my earliest formative self, and transports me by TARDIS to my happy place.

Alternative Translations of 'My Little Soul' by the Emperor Hadrian

The Latin Original

animula vagulia blandula
hospes comesque corporis
que nunce abibis? in loca
pallidula rigida nubila
nec ut soles dadis iscoes.

English

Little Soul, Little wanderer, charmed one
My body's guest and companion,
Where will you go to now? To places
Dark Lover, cold and gloomy
Where you won't tell any jokes.

Neath

You Casper, me little soul, like you know
Me old Butty and best Mate,
Where is you off to now like? To by there
Love, where it is absolutely minging.
You won't find it funny or any good see.

Klingon

Logl cH'e' Loq Wejpuh we
Lom meb je parmappy
Nug Day Qoch go chuglow? Dag
Meglc Hchaj we'bir, es, let
Dag Hug Dag, path boneH bomvaj tilbmsch.

Elvish

Dilthen facer, dilthen charmdder
Rancid nin bodiu's mellone malcthril
What na-cin quest? Dur malcthril
Thind echor a rovan
Whare cin shall treneri funnui tales.

Dalek

Mean low incorporeal entity
Vile Alien Intruder of my shell
You shall be Exterminated!
EXTERMINATED! EX-TER-MI-NAT-ED!

Ancient High Martian

Rrrrrrr, orrrrroooo, rippppttttt reeee
Clacker, Clacker click Briiiigining
Whoorrr, wherreee OOHpare? Pop POP
(Waving four tentacles) Waj Hoooommm LoWw HooMmmm
(Waving all eight tentacles) A looom RANNnnn Lext ta ta ta LooooooM.

Tracey Rhys

There's something so basic in the recognition you feel when you read a character who speaks as you speak. At ten years old I first came across it. In Maerdy Juniors School, a classmate rushed over from the class bookcase to show me the phrase 'I dunno' in a reading book she'd picked off the shelf. I made it my business to read it next.

Everything I'd got my hands on until this point had been designed to reinforce the rules of writing and spelling, but here we had a writer who gave their young readers credit for some big assumptions. We'd know that writing 'dunno' wouldn't get us through a spelling test. We'd know too that combining two words into one wouldn't get us a presenting job at the Beeb circa 1984, and we'd understand that this misspelling was functional. Whether slang or dialect, the portmanteau word 'dunno' tells us something about character, accent and upbringing that description doesn't quite capture. This character would be a bit like us: working-class and casually spoken. There's attitude there too—humour and spirit and aspiration and angst, depending on how they're offset by social, educational and political environments.

Later, when I was a young adult taking a Writing MA at Cardiff Uni in the '90s, some superb dialect writing dominated the era. James Kelman won the Booker Prize with *How Late it Was, How Late*, and everyone was already talking about Irvine Welsh after Trainspotting hit the big screen. A bit later, in Wales, John Williams' urban noir *Cardiff Trilogy* resonated with those of us living in the city. In the many poetry gigs of the era, Topher Mills and lloyd robson blazed with performances that played with both sound and speech, capturing place through voices in ways I'd never heard before.

In Cwmdare, a short drive over the mountain from my old primary school, Rachel Trezise probably convinced me most that there was a place for the Rhondda dialect in the canon of Welsh writing in English. Her memoir, *In and Out of the Goldfish Bowl*, was an uncompromising read. In its pages, our native dialect was as bold itself as her account of a damaged childhood was devastating.

Growing up, I'd seen us depicted on the stage in the packed-out comedies of Frank Vickery in the Parc and Dare theatre. The posters that my Nan stuck up in her window (she ran a bus trip for her friends to every one) claimed he'd 'brought the house down' and fair play, he did. The whole place reverberated with laughter from the back of the top circle to the front of the stalls. You could feel its rumble through the seats.

Because ... there we were! Us, our people, and we were hilarious. Hadn't we always known it? We were comic gold mun, us lot in the Valleys. We were tough and thoughtful and cruel and kind and just about as stubborn as mules. Easily led, mind. What better way to show this than in our own dialect? Our own tongue: as informed as any sharp-vowelled, long-consonanted writer. Sharper, even. There's a better view of the whole of society when you're standing at the bottom and looking up. What's there to argue with? Ey? Speak up!

Wish You Were Here

The TV tells my fortune.
Iss truths flicker like dreamz.
Fires inuh south. Floods inuh north.
An' the east coast 'ave disappeared,
crumblin into iss seaside fudge.
Most o' the time, I lissen yurr
like a ghost in a box
down in the front room
withuh fire off.
Out ina street,
exhausts are backfirin'
all hours o' the day an' night.
I carn gerw sleep, so I watch
the travel showz like I used to
whenuh kids were small
Wish You Were Here...?
with Judith Chalmers.
Only now, they're stormin'
the airport groundz,
an' th planes are riyzin'
with men on the wings.
An' the children are hidin'
behind biscuits tins
in the backs of artic trucks.

Anthracite

All the cold winter of '84,
we rummaged for coal at pit's top.
My God, woz like findin' gold itself,
each cob we threw into th'bucket.
Me an th'wife, th'kidz playin in th'dirt.
Sleet on our backs; i'was minus four.
Thar was the Chrissmas the city
started wearin' donkey jackets.
You got to laugh!
We 'ad become an icon o' fashun,
freezin' an' starvin an' beaten to an inch.
"Sufferin' is in," I sed to my butty.
Standin' an' fightin' is ever in vogue.

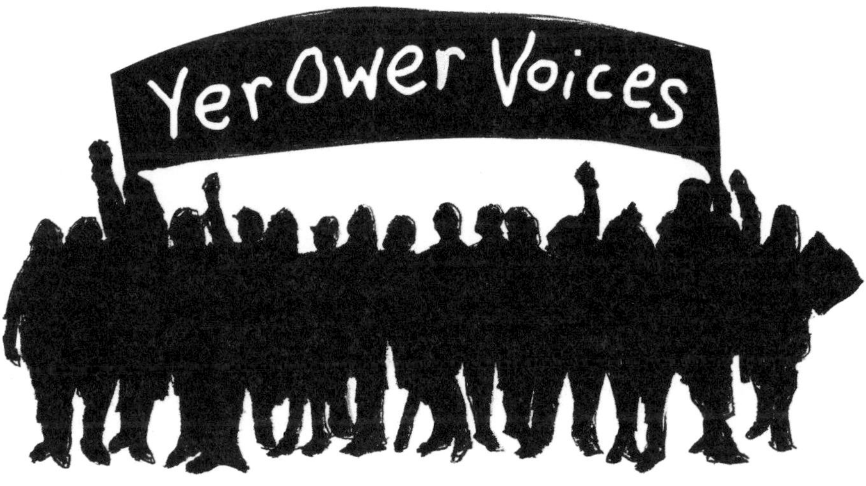

Mike Jenkins

I became fascinated by accents when my family moved from Aberystwyth to Cambridge when I was seven. I used to greet a lad from a 'rougher' part of the city walking to school in the morning and he'd reply—'Watcha mate!' To my west Walian ears this sounded like a threat.

But soon I got used to the quasi-Cockney, though far preferred the country accent when we moved to the border with Suffolk, so when I readily adopted it even my brawd would call me 'a yokel'!

It wasn't a great leap from rural East Anglia to embracing the characters of Hardy (who we studied at 'A' Level) and their Wessex dialect. Accent indicated class and also urban/rural dichotomies. In my grammar school there was a distinct three way divide—posh kids, city kids and us country ones, bused in from the sticks.

My first ever dialect poem was published in *Planet* when John Tripp was poetry editor. I was under the spell of Bob Marley at the time and 'Mr Management Man' was a long way from anything I was hearing in Barry, where I lived then.

A number of rivers met to change everything. Firstly, I moved to Merthyr where I taught at the Gurnos, at the top of a large council estate. Secondly. I was reading the likes of James Berry, Derek Walcott and listening to Linton Kwesi Johnson. Thirdly, I read (in *Planet*) the brilliant poem 'Swonzee Boy, See' by Dave Hughes.

Rivers met. Became one. Headed coastward and my first poem in Merthyr dialect, 'This Town', was heavily influenced by the Coventry ska band The Specials' single 'Ghost Town'. Remarkably, Derek Mahon took it for *The New Statesman*!

Nothing much has happened since then, save numerous volumes of poems and stories in that dialect. I have always tried to reflect its changes and also get closer to the sound, without impeding communication. For me, it's a vital part of my writing and I must thank one person especially, namely John Barnie, once editor of *Planet*. He set me on my way with his great encouragement and by publishing my first two books: *Graffiti Narratives* and *Could Bin Summin*.

I love the humour and energy of people I hear on the streets and buses. They do not deserve the oppression they have to endure daily in many cases, in a poor town in a country which is often an afterthought.

Girlz Carn Play

Girlz?
They carn play football!
More bothered 'bout make-up
an jewelree comin off,
theyer air disturbed,
theyer fake tans
messed up by bruisin.

Girlz?
All blydi lesbos anyway,
on'y geh involved
f'r-a changin rooms
an oo they fancy,
all affairs an intrigues
like *Eastenders* on fields.

Girlz?
Well, I aven actually seen
any of-a games on telly,
buh I cun imagine em
Doin theyer nails arf time.
blokes that watch em
mus' be dead pervie.

Oo Stole Ower Town?

Somebuddy stole ower town centre!
Some say it could be idden
up-a Retail, or stuck inside
them cardboard walls o Trago.
Others reckon it's bin taken
down t Cardiff, buh the buses
would never come t carry it.

Somebuddy stole ower town centre
coz the shops keep disappearin
an theyer emptee as Tory brains—
the piss-artists all bleeve
it's bin shifted underground
an fills the ol mines.

Somebuddy stole ower town centre
an now the Council's tryin t find
film companees with apocalyptic movies
oo're lookin f perfect settin's.
Oo nicked it....woz it Westmonster?
We're searchin f someone t blame
buh even-a Portuguese an Poles 're leavin.

Becomin A Woman

See, I wen f'r an interview
an they arst me
"Were you born a woman?"
I mean, ow blydi crazee—
tol em I wuz born a donkey.

Tha's wha they d' do nowadays.
I know this tidee bloke
ee become a woman,
ad the full op, didn ee?
Lovely fella, s'licitor an all.
Never slept with a woman.
Mind, some with kids
end up doin-a same.

Buh wha would appen
if I fancy im.....er?

Well, she've goh the equipment
down below, fitted proplee.

It's loop-the-loop,
sooner marry a donkey.

Yewer abits , I reckon
tha's far more likely.

Igh Sheriff o Merthyr

Ee wuz off of is trolley,
shoutin in-a middle o Penderyn Square
like ee woz a Town Crier.

Ee ad all the regalia—
chains, fancy at , medals galore,
buh ardly spoke posher.

"Yer ye, yer ye! Good folk o Merthyr!
I'm yewer bran'new Igh Sheriff
appointed arfta givin bagsomoney.

Ower good Queen 've sadly
passed away, wavin from-a sky
on a separate cloud to er ubby.

She ave served us mos graciously,
same time lookin arfta er famlee
(speshly er darlin son Andy).

Now we welcome King Charlie III
oo once spoke sev'ral words o Welsh
an loves talkin t trees.

We say 'Croeso!' t Wills ower prince
an look forward t showin im round
b'fore ev'ry business shuts down town.

As Igh Sheriff I yerby decree
Prince Charles becomes King Charles Ospital
An Keir Ardie Ealth Centre's named arfta Camilla.

As Igh Sheriff I yerby declare
this square will enceforth be named arfta me—
Josiah John Bacon Homfray Crawshay."

Fleein A Monster

She come on-a bus,
blood streamin down er face
from a gash on er fore'ead,
one black eye looked bard.

Somebuddy sayz—"Tha's the bes
Alloween make-up I seen yet!"
Then she bursts out cryin,
this woman give er a cwtsh.

"Whassa matter 'en love?"
"Ee've kicked me out!
Goin up my mam's I am.....
Witch ee sayz, geh on yewer broom!"

The blood run down er t-shirt,
somebuddy give er tissues.
No party f'r er tonight,
fleein a real monster.

This bloke gehs on at-a Club,
scars an stitches, all kindsa stuff.
Nobuddy sayz nothin, as-a girl
olds er ead an weeps.

My eatin policy

Is stoppin in bed all day long—
I aven done tha
since my oneymoon.
Buh now the missis ave gone
my on'y compnee
is the television.

Down town apparently
they goh summin called
an Eatin Bank,
it's where Wilko ewsed t be,
some fancy name like Talkin Shop.

Made my will the other day—
my ouse'll go t pay
f me in an Ome.
Sometimes it feels
like this bed's a comfy coffin
when all my joints pain an stiffen.

My kids goh me a mobile—
fair play they do ring
t check if I'm still livin—
"I've moved t Bedford"
I tell em an they larf
with "See yew soon!"

Ey Mister Lan'lor'

Tell me, Mister Lan'lor'
wha yew doin t me?
Jest me an my kid
tryin t make ends meet.

I work like a dog
a collie chasin sheep,
I'm on yewer leash.
Carn afford no car,
train fares always goin up,
food prices beyond
'lectric's the same—
yew wan' us t end
up on-a street?

Ey Mister Lan'lor'
I know yew gotta make money,
buh yew goh more ouses
than I goh GCSEs
an I done tidee
even though I work in Tragos.

Yew ever gone without?
Gone to a foodbank?
Secon' thoughts I'm more like a sheep,
with yew snappin us inta pens.
Wha's-a fewture, eh?
Some ewman blydi abbatoir?

Leigh Manley

My initial encounter with dialect writing arrived while studying at Aberystwyth University in the mid-1990s; the fictional prose of Glaswegian novelist James Kelman appearing on the reading list. At the time, as far as I was concerned, the closest a 'Welsh' creative had come to delivering anything similar was down to a nebulous link with another Scottish novelist in the process of assuming his rightful place in UK popular culture through his cult classic, *Trainspotting*. It seemed to me, as a Welsh Anglophone, that, as far as writing in dialect was concerned, there was Scottish English, even 'Scottish Welsh', but a distinct absence of Welsh English.

It was 2022 before I stumbled across lloyd robson's collection, *cardiff cut* (first published in 2001). Later that year, I became increasingly aware of dialect poetry being shared by Mike Jenkins out of Merthyr. For me, this coincided with *Poetry Wales* announcing an issue with a focus on the potential of Cymraeg, possibly imagining contributions in Welsh English dialects. Just weeks later, Mike issued an invitation for submissions to a possible anthology of poetry from across the spectrum of Welsh dialects. I thought to myself, 'Quality! I've gorra give i' a butchers!'

As you may have just guessed, my own dialect writing is of a 'Valleys' persuasion, influenced by the collective voice of my upbringing in Maesteg. I've been careful to avoid the temptation to cite the dialect as being more specific to the Llynfi Valley, for fear of all manner of misrepresentations.

Herein lies just one of the difficulties of writing poetry in dialect, conspicuous as it is for its absence in being captured on the page on a scale. Vincent van Gogh supposedly said, 'poetry surrounds us everywhere, but putting it on paper is, alas, not so easy as looking at it.' How about throwing in the additional complexity of analysing the pronunciations one may be familiar with hearing but unaccustomed to seeing written down? There's also the fluid nature of all language, shifting as it does with the passage of time, movements of people, technological advancements.

Nevertheless, I found the warts 'n' all purity of writing in dialect made accessible a humour I find difficult to uncover when writing in standard English, whilst somehow the language itself encouraged me not to take myself too seriously; a liberating experience when writing. Though ostensibly contradictory to the previous point, there's also the weight of history, a consciousness the world should be moving towards greater equality, a fear it's not; a determination to at least lend my fledgling poetic voice to a more diverse and inclusive literary landscape.

Warren Eader

Bloody 'ell!
Ee's on'ee gone 'n come back mun.
'Bonkers!' Boys 'r sayin.
Reckon ee's off his trolley
Lost-a plot big time!

Carn gerray 'ead round why
Ee'd pur is neck on-a line agen
Arfta all 'em Gran Slams.
Thumpa sez ee's bin on tha wacky baccy.

Carcass reckons ee's jus skint like.
Says is Nana clocked im drivin
Buses up Nanty las week: knew i was im
Cos i' was Edwards Coaches. I dunno bow tha.

Muggins by yuh reckons ee shoulduv
Give Shaun a tinkle before jumpin onboard.
I told im ee'd already signed with-a Frogs
Bur ee weren avin any of i'.

Jus kep sayin warren 'eader ee was
Thinkin ee could turn a-mess around,
How tha Yewnyun soon be sellin Gatland
Wallpaper to ide tha cracks.
I doan wanna go down tha 'ole.

Fa whar'is worth,
I'm chuff't t'bits ee's back:

Knows us berra than we know
Arselves, ee do.
Ivor tha, or ee's gorra crystul ball:
Named is son Bryn after all.
And ee'll tackle evreething 'ead on.

If anyone can pull a rabbit
Ourra tha warren...

Uppa Bird

Did yew know Kylie's arf-Welsh?
'Er Nana was a Jones mun. True ar-is.
When I wuz a nippa
Gazette run-a story reglar on uh.
Stonkin she was. Still is mun.
I oft'n majin'd I wuz 'er neighbour
instead-a tha pew-nee Donovan bloke.
She made my top ten evree single time
Up-air on fit lists wiv Sara and Bethan and Siân.
If she'd lived in-a vallee, all-a boys would-a
Warnid to ger off wiv 'er. Naw shaw ow
She'd ave gorron uppa Bird-o, wiv all-a
Strutters, nutters, n'slappers-a buttocks;
Catfights, scraps, 'n' starin at baps.
Don' know ow I'd-a coped eeva.
Or copped? I'm a luva nor-a fighta.
Ev'n now, I jes carn gerra out-a my 'ead.
Saw 'er on-a telly thee other day
Told-a missus straight like:
I'd dew tha loco-motion with 'er awright.
She took-a drag on 'er fag, said,
'I should be so lucky,'
Wharever tha'sposed t'mean?

Dead Good Egg

Iss so ard t' believe ee's gone, poor dab.
I feels fir is mutha—findin im outta back
Like at—musta broke er art.
Such a luvlee boy, such a good lookin lad.
Iestyn fought an awful lot of im, ee did,
Said ee wuz-a life 'n' soul; liked a swig
'N ta dabble witha powda, but wouldn'
Arm a fly like, said ee was a dead good egg.
On'ee jus gor out too. Such a pitee.
Is dad was tellin Uw tha iss sum consulay-shun
To is mutha t' know ee's 'ome fir good now
'N she cun keep 'n eye on im when she's
Doin er weedin or angin outta washin.

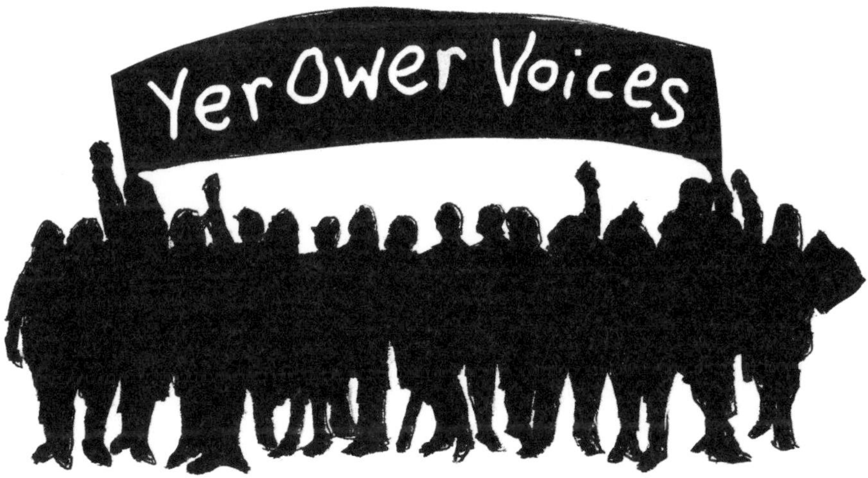

Kitty Jay

When not hiding behind her pseudonym and writing poems, Kitty Jay can usually be found squirrelling away in her lady-cave researching obscure facts about the Roman Empire or visiting castles hyd a lled Cymru. Desperately trying to make her first million before the age of 90, she has her 'Welsh castles jigsaw collection' venture to fall back on if her debut poetry book 'Running on Empty' goes down like a lead balloon. 'Wossa Point Mun?' was inspired by negative attitudes and comments from an uncomfortable number of pupils in Blaenau Gwent schools towards learning Welsh as a second language.

Wossa Point Mun?

'Wossa point o learning Welsh, Miss?
Iss no' gonna be any yewss t me
Wen I leev skool!'

'Wossa point o learnin' Welsh, Miss?
Nobuddy do speak it in Gwent like—
Rownd yer, thee Inglish langwidge do rool!'

'Worra bout yew 'en, Lowri ler?
Yew yewsed t go t Welsh skool
B4 u woz yer in comp wiv us!'

'It woz 'ard an I hated 'em teachers
Bu' Langrannog woz cool
Singin at th back o the bus!'

'Lowri hates Welsh, an' all, see Miss!
Iss minging, pointless innit,
S'no fun!'

'My farther agrees butt, I tell 'ew—
Learn Welsh like? He do laugh! He do go,
"Wossa point mun?!" '

Jenny Sullivan

I write in Welsh dialect usually, possibly because I live in Brittany and suffer (badly) from hiraeth. I've occasionally used a Cockney dialect and sometimes a "posh" one—but usually only disrespectfully. My mother was pure BBC English and tried to make me the same. I needed camouflage in primary school so my accent suited situation or company. Talking posh was a good way to get duffed over! Sometimes I slipped up at home: "I never done nothin'" usually earned me a clip round the ear—and eventually elocution lessons. I've also used Irish—see below.

Some of my 15 "Magic Apostrophe" children's novels feature a leprechaun, O' Liam of the Green Boots, who loves an Irish proverb so HAD to beportrayed in dialect! The Welsh heroine and her family—well, I don't use dialect, but they have Welsh speech patterns and intonation. I hope....

The characters in my books identified themselves; I wrote their speech as they told me! For poetry, sometimes it's the only way to get the feel for the poem's narrator. It's important to give a sense of place, character and social status. All parts of Cartref Cymru have their own dialect and intonation.

Difficulties? Some years ago my publisher since 1994 decided to quit. I couldn't face trying to find another, so I've been using Amazon Createspace, editing my own work.

Rewards? I've had published around 31 novels for adults and children and many short stories and poems in anthologies—but the financial rewards were subsidised by a day job. The greatest rewards have been the eight nominations for the Tir na n-Og Award, and winning it twice. However, it would have been impossible to survive without my husband's support.

"Llydaw" is basically about being somewhere beautiful—and still wishing I was in Wales instead. My favourite lines are "Friendly, look—well/Long as yewer p'lite first, any'ow!" because this sums up not only the Bretons but also the Welsh.

My Londoner Dad could identify an East End accent at fifty paces. So: parochial. Universal? A Welsh accent—from anywhere—makes me sit up and beg —especially when I hear one in Llydaw!

Llydaw

Iss a luvly country, wara teg
Green, like, an' nice rivers an' stuff
An' nobody do drop litter nowhere.
Nice flowers inna towns
An' they don' get vand'lised nor nicked, neither.
Good like tha', the Bretons.

Theyer orright, too
Friendly, look—well,
Long as yewer p'lite first, any'ow!

Celtic, see, like us.
Weather's the same—
On'y—well, the rain's warmer.

I should be dead 'appy by yer, right?
Luvly it is.
'Ceptin'
Well, it in't Wales, is it?
Iss not *'ome.*

I think they d' call it "eeraeth".

Lorraine Voss

I was born in Aberdare General Hospital in 1964. My father came from Hirwaun and was the son of a cobbler. My mother was from a Merthyr coal mining family. We lived in Hereford, Penarth and Penderyn before settling in Ebbw Vale in 1968. This is where I was formed.

I won my first prize for poetry in 1973 at Pont y Garreg Primary School in the Rassau. It was called The Postman and I can still recite it now.

In recent years I've won Eisteddfod prizes for poetry and short stories at Llanwrtyd Wells, Trallong, Painscastle, Upper Chapel and Llanafan Fawr. The most recent prizes were for works written in Wenglish.

The poems included in this anthology are my first attempt at writing in South Wales Valleys dialect. The influence for this came from a Facebook post by Mike Jenkins asking for submissions of this kind. Before seeing this post it had never occurred to me to write the way I speak, or more accurately, spoke!

While writing the poems I realised just how many words have fallen from my common use, I think this is in some part due to the passing of time—some words just get left behind or become unfashionable. I also think that when I moved from the Valleys to Mid Wales in 2008 my dialect and accent gradually morphed as a way to tuck me into my new location comfortably. I felt that when in Rome, I should at least aim to speak Italian. The alternative was to forever be referred to as 'Her, from off.'

The process of writing these dialect poems has been fascinating and far more psychologically impactful than I would have anticipated. Although the actual Valleys words returned with ease, I found it almost impossible to write anything set in the here and now. All I could do was write from the perspective of the me who spoke those words in that specific time and place. For me, the poems feel very much like old photographs.

I Do Do

I do do sewin I do
Mam, teached me how to.
I cwd tern up yewer trouzers
an youd never even tell.

I cun shorten jackit sleeves
put a new zip in them jeans;
elastics in thah shell suit.
and taper yewer bell (bottoms).

An I wouldn charge you much butt
cuz I know youm always skint
an I know if I say 15 quid
you'll jus say 'Effin ell'.

So I'm chargin you a fiver
un I don't expect that eyethuh!
'A favour for a favour?'
Oh go on en; Might as well.

Goppin'

Aww flippin eck mun
youm doin my ed in.
I told yew I'm noh comin out.

Buh wossnim is waitin
down by thu bus stop.
I told im I'd give ew a shout.

You shouldunnav told im nuffin,
yew muppet!
Yew shouldunnav mucked im about.

He thinks we'll be snoggin;
We won't coz he's goppin!
So tell im, I ent comin out.

Reemaaarrkaaabul!

—Cardiff & Newport

Tôpher Mills

'I was Cardiff born and Cardiff bred and when I dies I'll be Cardiff dead.'

When Frank Hennessey sang those lyrics his was the only voice on TV and Radio that spoke with a genuine Cardiff accent. The only other places you heard it was in the working-class areas of Cardiff. I grew up in Grangetown and I still live there, two doors away from the house I was born in. I was, and am, surrounded by a multiculture of languages and dialects from around the world and they all seemed to meld into one distinctive local accent/dialect.

There are differences to the way people in different areas speak. A word like mate, or for most of Wales, butty (where the Americans get 'buddy' from), is different in different parts of Cardiff. East of the Taff in Roath, Splott and Adamsdown, they say 'skip' (as in 'how's it going skip' or 'give us a hand with this skip'). In the docklands, Butetown etc., they say 'Bra' or 'Bro'. South of the Taff, Grangetown, Riverside, Canton and Ely, they say 'spar', as in 'he's my spar he is' (coming from the boxing term 'sparring partner'). These days, with everyone moving around a lot, these terms are no longer so well defined in their regions.

Before I'd thought of writing a dialect poem I'd heard the likes of Stanley Holloway, Pam Ayres and John Cooper Clarke, who were not dialect poets but their regional accents played a definite part in their work. Then there were the dub poets like Mikey Smith, Linton Kwesi Johnson and locals Martin Glynn, Mickey Coulam and Nicky Delgado. I also encountered the Canadian dialect poet Bill Bissett who, like e.e. cummings, had invented a language of his own. I would wonder what my poetic language/voice was?

One day I saw the irascible Ian McMillan read a send-up of a Yorkshire dialect poem. It was very funny and I wondered if I could do a mock Cardiff dialect poem. I began collecting words peculiar to Cardiff. Almost two years later there were a lot of words but no poem. Then I went to see the great Glaswegian dialect poet Tom Leonard, who was touring South Wales, and, like a lot of other local writers, I was a positively inspired. His poems and a brilliant essay he wrote, made me realise that I should take the dialect seriously.

I wrote the first Cardiff dialect poem, 'Nevuh Fuhget Yuh Kaairdiff', and having done that had no intention of writing more. However as other poets, some also inspired by Tom Leonard, started writing dialect poems, I found myself responding to and inspired by their poems. Writers like Dave Hughes, Irene E.

Thomas and Mike Jenkins were at the forefront of this. These writings brought working-class languages and speech patterns into poetry and this helped me find both my language and my voice as a working-class poet.

Reemaaaarrkaaabul

(*uh Kaairrdiff lullaabi*)

Bedtiem 'Jaabberwocky'
sendin duh Saandmaan
tuh clowz lidul uzzuks iez
wid staardust sprinkul

tuh fli sleep intuh dreem
beefower dyh ate o clok
monstur prowels duh laandin
sniffin owt duh waykful

redee tuh drink duh blud
uh duh refewgees uv nod
so if yoos bee preetendin
faaik it flaabertaaastikaly

bee comaa ded tuh dis wirld
aan duh neksd, paancaaik flaat
coopeed in duh caasul dunjun
in duh deepist minds mien

waandrin paast Laarnog Poyunt
aarn dowun bee trikd bi im
tikin liek graampees waatch
liek ees gor uh faairee storee

aaskin aakword kwestuns
liek Klaaarksee or Paaarksee?
(dats aalwayz aal aakordin)
Baazzee Ieelund or Aaaleekaantee?

keep yuh gorpurs shut tiet
if is golum tung raasps yuh tows
doh ir tikuls dowun daair skwirm
jes fink uv eetin cheeez on towsd

aarn wen ut laasd ee uv skaarpurrd
yoo kaan waarmlee snugul dowun
tuh sleep duh widee snooozez
dreem uv pit pownees praancin

raaaftin on duh river Taaaf
bee em eks bunee opin duh baaraaj
skofin Dorofees orf duh bone
kuryd chiken an lowdsa chips

levitayt frum Caarolien street baak
tuh duh graaing end wid tumee ful
yoo wul kip til mornin fiends yoo
dedo an snorin sumting maaavelus!

Angin Abowt

ee's up there
makin the roof
'more betterer' (ee laughs)
I'm down ere
catchin raindrops
gobbin on earwigs
watchin em curl up
that ole cement bucket
risin on the orange rope
to im up there
doin I doan know what
the flashin on the chimney
nailin the odd slate on

searchin for the screwdriver
what ee's been sat on an then
avin to go back up
the moved ladder to get it

sat on the wall
under the tree
backs to the hedge
well out of the rain
ee passes me a Welsh mint
as the late lunches
come out of The Beverley
the pavement all dug up
traffic jammin
that lorry flattenin those bollards
we laugh at the navvies
swearin at the clerks
behind their thin backs
especially one dozy lookin git
in a yellow plastic mac

"ee's a university tyke
knows bugger all about it I'll bet
tryin to teach em their job, christ!
dey knows more than ee'll ever know"
"aye" I replies, lookin at
that sore dark spot
where I jammed my thumb
between two sections of gutterin
to rediscover the agony
an the racism
of a 'black man's pinch'

ee gets up to go back on top
it's not really rainin now
an my thumb's stopped throbbin
ee looks at me, smiles
"university!

that's where dey
takes yuh brains out yur ead
an shoves em up yur arse init?"

Buying Shares in the Jobcentre

"I been ovuhdrawn now fuh almost for yers
an no way uh payin it off liek.
Des always dat unakownted bil, yewno
dee gas, lectric or me onlee luksuree, duh fown.
I carn fink ow jus livin
kun so eeklips me inkum liek
I doan smowk or drink uh loh
an no waze um I uh bludee fashun viktim
an as fuh eggsortik fuwds liek
yew no, I aven bort uh stayk
in wel ovuh uh yer now!
Bakun offkuts, dass me onlee reggewla meet
nor frew tyoiss miend buh eekonomiks.
Wah wif dee impropuh dieyat
an naf orl entuhtaynment
(evun seks iz kostlee)
les fayss it, lief's aardlee wurf livin izit?
Ger uh job dey sez, urn uh few bob
buh jeezus ders no wurk iz zeh?
Pettee kryim, fiduls, evun a weeks onnest
o yeh, orl uh dart, buh nor reel wurk liek
fullee payeed, taksd an inshored an nat
yoo's godda bee kidin!
Duh blak maarkits dee ownlee fing
dass keepin Fatyurz paradice gowin init!
If ownlee I new wear ir wuz gowin?
Orl I noes fuh shor iz
iss nor gowin mi bluddee way izit?"

The Last Drunk in the Pub

aav yews eva bin in luuv
wid sumwon oo luuvs anuduh
nowin deyul nevuh bee yowers
pienin koz dey uh wid anuduh

aav yews eva felt daat payun
duh sikunin won dat nors
tyernin yuh insieds
klorin at duh baak uh yuh frowt

aave yews eva kurst yuhself
hert flowin liek aassid rayun
felt trew lownleenus swolo yew up
mayd uh room emptee biee yuh presuns

aav yews eva kurst def
koz ir kud wiep owt eevun luuv
aytid orl forts koz dey no
der won way owts too eezee

aav yews eva endluslee eksplaynd tuh yuhself
wiee yews doan reeuhlee luuv dem
aow yewul ger ova dem in tiyum
dow eevun deyur sheeaado berns

aav yews eva bitun yuh tung
aan wundud wiee der ownlee fing yew feeyuls
iz zaat dey aar nort wif yoo
luuv nulifiyin orl udun payun

aav yews eva sufud wen dey didunt corl
kerst an swor an aytid dem an yuhself
ownlee tuh bee instuntlee apee at der voys
til dey tels yew dey doan luuv yew

aav yews eva.......................

Kaairdiff Maarkit

In Kaairdiff Sentrul Maarkit init
trayps weyuh maybee baarginz sit
broarn, haaslit, ofkuts uv Pershun caarpit
reediskoverrd rekord uv uh paast hit
kayjez wer smellee haamstirs skwit
toyee stol plaastik ayerfiks caar kit
sekond aand buks uv faymus maan's wit
fuh ful brekee speshul den sit
soopa strawng saamovaar cuppa tyar it
yor playt awaayts duh paan hit
see seetid kidz aavin uh laafin fit
beenz orn towst or welsh raairbit
joowelerz waatj dayer waatjis tik
bootjerz, baakuhz, haabaadaashuz nit
vintaaj wayst kowts, haats daat fit
froot aan vej, fowns, uh warkin stik
eelektrikalz, guttid fish, haair redee plaatid
brik uh brak uh bit uv taat fuh tit
ieeon trusd glaaysd rewf, slaats shayd it
ayr lit sumuh sun shimuz, wintuh staar lit
owld clok tayks orl ower tiem aan maarkz it
daatz Kaairdiff Sentrul Maarkit init.

Nevuh Fuhget Yuh Kaairdiff

Fraank Fanaarkaapaanz on duh mitch
inis bestest daps
onis faastest underaang bogey
like uh propuh Beano comic

Mad Motters donkeyin
raaysin froo Grange-end gaardns
korzin uh wopin grate malaarkee
dodgin duh dideekoys

scraamblin kross duh daafs
kraakin jelly froo duh tyewlips
an nuh Paarkeez frowin uh woblee
totuley owta duh winda like

"BLUDY LIDUL DOWZOWS"
ee yelz all jottld up to is nodjem
"YEWUL GET SUM GROLUP YEW ERVA
PAARKS YUR AARS ROWUND YUR AGEN"

Motter mite be beejobuld
buh Fanaakaapaan ees norra dill
iss is dreem wen ee growz up
tuh bee obuldeeoy tuh duh kween

aan duh Paarkeez aad uh maajorum
is germojumz gon all maankee
"Faaraawaakin boluhwoks" ee baars
"iyum orf down duh skin ows"

aark aark duh laark
frum Kaairdiff aarms paark
iyull aav uh Klaarksee pi
aan un aarf aan aarf uh Daark
aa aan
uh baanaanuh jaam saarnwidj

A Child's Christmas in Cardiff

I WANTS A BMX BIKE!
I WANTS A BMX BIKE!
I WANTS A BMX BIKE!

aan iss krissmuss morning
aan gess wot?

I GORRA BMX BIKE!
I GORRA REEL BMX BIKE!
I GORRA BMX BIKE!

aan duh furst fing I dus on it
is I tayuks ir owt duh layun
aan I doos dis faaantaaastik weeelie
aan I forls orf
aan I lans on mi bum
aan I urts myself
aan I kries
WAAAAAAAAAAAAAAAAAAAAAAAAAAAA!
aan mummi kums aan gets mee
WAAAAAAAAAAAAAAAAAAAAAAAAAAAA!
aan kaarrees mee baak in dee ows
WAAAAAAAAAAAAAAAAAAAAAAAAAAAA!
aan kudduls mee
WAAAAAAAAAAAAAAAAAAAAAAAAAAAA!
aan kissus mee bettur
                    YEEUURK!

Aaan now
I gorra BMX bike
                    fuh sayul!

Peter Finch

Peter Finch is a poet based in Cardiff, Wales. Both of those places feature heavily in his verse.

lloyd robson once famously declared "I write in the Cardiff Language"—he meant in Cardiff, the street tongue of the capital, as opposed to in Welsh, the older tongue of this country—which I guess is what I do when I need to. Poets write in a range of registers and for me local speech patterns are just one of the things I have in my arsenal. The Welsh language, one of the great influences on Cardiff speech despite denial in some quarters, is another. *Partisan*, included in this anthology, is macaronic, mixing English vernacular with Welsh pretty much as how it often is in some parts of the city where speakers flicker from one language to the other without pause.

Kerdif Cairdiffe, part of which is engraved in the paving outside the central library on The Hayes in Cardiff, started as a sort of concrete poem which blended the mad variety of ways the name for the city had been spelt in documents since documents began. The work spun in to mix Cardiff dialect, Welsh and Latin (with leanings towards Norman French) much as speech might have centuries ago—"quid est? beth yw hwn? what is this?" The road signs back then, if they'd had them, would have been huge.

Why do I engage in this? Ezra Pound's imperative was that we poets should constantly seek to make it new. Employing dialect and macaronics certainly aids in the quest to do that.

Is any of this important? In a world where written speech is heading fast towards a digital universal, yes it is. This is who we are and, on the street, how we often speak. Language changes at a rapid rate. It always has done. Writing it down gives it both respectability and strength.

Dialect writing isn't new. William Barnes wrote in Dorset in the nineteenth century. Tennyson in Lincolnshire. Robbie Burns amazed us in Scots, virtually a language in itself. But kind of writing is still underrated. Standard English and formal Welsh always gets you to places that street slang won't. But poetry, thank God, changes. The arrival of new languages and speech inflection in Wales is aiding the shift. There might be a few battles up ahead but then poetry should be used to that.

Peter Finch's Collected Poems *appeared in two volumes from Seren last year.*

Partisan

rydw i am fod blydi I am
rydyn ni rydw i rody i
rodney rodney I am
rydyn am fod I am I am I am
rydw i yn Pantycelyn Rhydcymerau Pwllheli yes

I am bicupping mainly cym sticker aardvark
the dictionary cymro hirsute weirdo
on fire arrested finger-pointed rydych chi
imperialist long-nosed pinky cottagers

roeddwn i'n fine yn y bore oherwydd
y heddlu not able anyway little zippo
lager considerable influence
tried to burn it not enough alcoalcohol
corner shop four-pack Diamond White Red Stripe
brns your heart out

rudin wedi dysgu hen ddigon ol' moulderin
Welsh Saunders Mabinognog crap
nasty blydi books   we're a video neishyn
smot superbod sam tan brilliant example

ac yn nawr?
bod ar y satellite no defence
carchar poms yn saesneg
dim yn gallu handlo'r cymraeg
rîl traditional blydi Welshman.

Kerdif

Dŵr Caerdydd mate
pal aright skip
Cocks Tower Tŵr
bibles henges fish
imprisoned recidivist Rawlins
right White matey mate

Milkmaid Hayes Waterloo Bridge
Glam canal
ditch and flumen
Taf floodplain flud
pont point pint port pwynt

Sabrina Afon Hafren
Severn solid
Sandy Roman frith

Kerdif Cairdiffe

quid est?
beth yw hwn?
what is this?

Greyhound Spice Box antiquarian
Huxley's surgical goods
embiggened bog shoreline sunk
alluvial gravel buried books
wall and garden   canal ley

Russell Dunleavy Jack Brooks
Bute Wood Hugh Despenser
John Batchelor Llywelyn Bren
Shirl Vic Billy Dannie Frank
Gilbert de Clare John Cory Mary Clark
Tosh Billy Raybould Terry Nation

Thrasher Box Stockdale Superted
Jim Driscoll Mike Harries Peg-the-Wash
Billy-my-Stick Hairy Mick
Cochfarf Dammy Sammy
Bin-banger Ninjah Toy Mic Trevor

Psychic centre south Cardiff
y man lle mae'r pŵer yn cwrdd
place where the power seeps

Near this spot you could once
cross a Cardiff bridge
before that a Norman ditch
then Welsh water
then Roman mud

Was there much here
found in the clay?
socketed axe head
with converging ribs
bone fragment pot
a few microliths

Now all lost

Colin Baker Dr Who
1986 time capsule
didn't find this

Future future
Llên Caerdydd Cardiff shine
Cardiff books Empty Caerdydd bricks

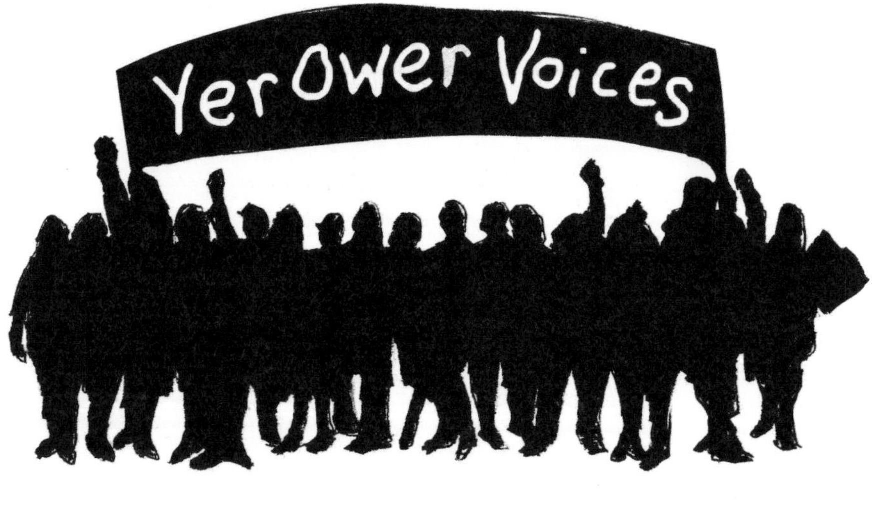

Mab Jones

I sometimes write in the Cardiff / Kerdiff accent / dialect, as that's where I'm from. My mother's family in particular speak with a strong city accent. It's one way I've found of making my mum laugh: I drop into accent and use dialect like 'argy bargy' and 'aggro', mocking and teasing her a little each time.

The Cardiff accent is very broad-sounding, with a lot of wide, elongated vowels—Keeeeerdiff—which give an association of 'lowness'. There's an assumption that people with a strong Cardiff accent are lower class and stupid. Since I'm from that class myself—the stratum of people for whom work is a must, but the circumstances of birth mean that usually only low-paid work is possible—I know that there's a link, but intelligence shouldn't come into it. So, this is one of the challenges of this accent and dialect—class association, and the associations of class.

Dialect words usually exaggerate the accent and add to that sense of the speaker being a bit of a 'duppuh'. I know that poet Liz Berry has done work reclaiming the Black Country accent and dialect in her poems, transmuting 'low' to 'high'. But I'm not sure this is possible with Kerdiffian, and she had *Peaky Blinders* to help her. Who have we got? Nessa from *Gavin & Stacey*, I suppose, who's shrewd at times, but also portrayed as a clown, a sidekick, and 'un-feminine'.

Recent poems I've written could probably be described as feminist, in that they emulate sexist views I've heard expressed. In the accent, with dialect, these views seem less intelligent, more stupid. So, I'm using what I've got—this inherited tongue—to try and change views, but in a different way to Berry.

Another difficulty with this accent is there's no accepted way to really write it. I'm in a lineage of Kerdiff dialect writers, and they all seem to spell things differently. I'm influenced by Peter Finch's experimentation with these words, morphing even one spelling, in some instances, into countless difference, like a weird Welsh Wordle; but I also love Topher Mills' pithy glimpses into everyday working-class life. They both incorporate humour, Kerdiff accent / dialect seems to invite it. But as a woman I can't help bringing my own experience to it, too.

A lot of dialect words in the Kerdiff accent express actions and processes like fighting, throwing up, having strong emotions and sensations. They're a rich vein for a poet to plumb. I don't know if writing in dialect is parochial or universal, but the richness of regional dialect is to be celebrated, for sure.

Ida no

Ida no. Ida no
wye ere iz.
Buh. Buh. Eye
gore uh gud
eye dear.

Oo nose,
tho, reelly.
Eye doughn.
Oo reelly nose.
Eye dough no
oo nose.

Gaw, i'slike—
no wun gorruh
cloo. Tho sum
preet endz they
do, lyke.

Eye goh mighown
thirts onnih. Buh
eye kud beerong.

I jusdoe no.
N'offer shure.
Ju?

lloyd robson

i am (or have been) a poet, prose writer, journalist, broadcaster, and text artist. i have often written in my own voice. i come from Cardiff, so i have written in a Cardiff dialect—not the epitome of 'the' Cardiff dialect (there is no single, set dialect) but in my voice. it's a very honest, textured, and musical way of speaking, and writing. it seemed like a natural and obvious choice to make.

letter from sissi (an extract)

you're aware of tha drill: daddy beard, mummy quiet, longhaired lolita and ugly academic child takin up tha frontrow of tha bus, tuggin tha blind down so no one except themselves can see what tha fuck's goin on (noisy, obnoxious, allknowin as well).

each member of this family had their topnotch boxbrownie an insteada jus takin tha picture they wanted/refusin ta snap til they discussed it fuh ages so all of us could listen (this one a primetime wish not to be british, i puts it down toa lacka inhibition/overeducation in the upmarket 'english' way).

the bus still bombin i wears me imperial stare as if they would care an tune inta their victorian conversation:

"Father, do you require a spare roll of film?"

"No, I do not require a spare roll of film,
why, do you have one?"

at which i was prayin the son would reply with:

"what a stupid fuckin question."

or pull out some:

"well tough fuckin shit then."

if his dad had been needin but the twat fucked it befor it got goin (his father controllin even when coastin) the sproggy little shit merely answerin:

"Well *yes*, actually."

can you believe it? (the lord blessed in his brothel) i thought we had bottle/ lived in tha twentieth century, obviously i'm well offline but modern man i'm sure has learnta rhyme what he needs to say with a certain eee-con-nno-mee/ without revertin to tha crime of adoptin a victorian style while still getting the message across witha:

"waniss?"

"no ta"

"thass fine"

nothin could be simpler, *nowaimean*?
such clarity of communication.

punchin out tha lights

i cums ome & yude left
so i got wrecked

& ended up, no, *wished*
tha caught ina corna of me eyelids

yor yellow lamp/existence ina corna of aar livin space
would stop iss fidgetin:

anglehead ta floor
perched precarious ona Wharfedale ™ & bouncin tha door

peekin iss halo rim

towards me

        & i wuz NOT seein things
        it wuz *movements*:

anklenips froma screwfit subjected ta gravity
flickers strobin a thousandyard intensity

        punches rainin froma dancin heavyweight conspiracy
        sliteyed & promisin ta get me

so i wuz boxed to me corna again
wi an unnervin seizure a territory

        i hadta snap outa & rapidstyle
        4tha sake a me sanity

so blinked
& lefta fucka ta wobble, til

        i hadta growl:

“one more step, one more fuckin step, & there’s
more grief than yu can andle, more shit than yu can shake pal
righ! thassit! thass fuckin it tha is!”

        & i pummels the lamp for iss trouble
        waste ofa fuse but i won the battle

but seemingly not the war.
but don’t worry my love, i can wait

        until yu
        gess ome.

wait
til yu
gess home....

words undeserving

scram
cree
listen sonny
sarky git
a right spiv
dirty stop-out
hussy
gallivant
charabanc
leave it out
cor blimey
Uncle Tom Cobbly
absa-bleedin-lootlee
short arms, deep pockets
who's minding the shop, Morry?
wazz, slash
spacky daps
fuckin Joey Deakin
fair do's
can't knock it
wouldn't touch her with yours.

a curious pace (an extract)

the A.
the O A.
the Old Arc
aid: bread pudding soaking up daytime pints, betting shop pens give up on wet Echoes. a loser backed & a cocked-up crossword.

"ya daft a'puth"
"ya dozy born bastard"

"the thing is..."
—"my arse!"

a right piccalilli.
arguing the toss.
waking up in the night to dance the Brains Dark trot.

the brewery gone. the Albert closed. Caroline divorced, in sunder, cleft, hewn, carved, sliced, chipped even, fractured & fractionised by the number-crunch hosts. frontline between the Brewery Quarter & the old alf-n-alf you do the math & i'll pick the bones. Dorothy's world-famous chicken curry or a soupçon of pretension served on a bed of sweet rocket with a drizzle of balsamic vinaigrette, extra-virgin olive oil or fresh basil sauce. hmmm, doan sound half bad when yungry. stick one a them in a crusty cob then, sweetheart & i'll take it ome. portion a chips an all. & a tub a curry sauce. growing boi, see. woan do no arm. no. no.

wrappers booted at passing cabs or spilt on the street.
John Batchelor doan get to eat no more.

Adam Street rapists, muggers on Black Bridge, verbal hurled from the bars of Knox Road. schoolkids giggling on gravestones, the smell of wet trees by the magistrates' court. Sunday planned & prepared on the dark walk home: a pint in the Clifton & listen to Elvis, a lamb dinner at Tony's, watch football, get stoned. not too bad as weekends go.

Mary Kaye

I write in a Cardiff dialect because, as Frank Hennessey sings, "I'm Cardiff born, Cardiff bred." I love the accent too, which is an advantage as my speech has a definite Caaardiff twang!

The first dialect poem I recall reading was *The Collier's Wife* by D.H. Lawrence, which intrigued me, particularly as it echoes issues relating to the coal industry of South Wales. Welsh dialect poets who have influenced me include Mike Jenkins, Topher Mills and Gemma June Howell.

I find that poetry written in dialect can express more powerfully the essence of a poem where the key themes, should they be written 'proper' would be lost. *Inni luv*, for instance, would read very differently and its impact lost without the use of dialect:

"Like the caastle's great an all tha
no denyin an' the aarcades aar unique"

versus

"Like the castle's great and all that
no denying and the arcades are unique"

Writing in dialect means that the usual rules of spelling and grammar need not apply and it's freeing to be able to pen poems without such constraints. The same line would be dull:

"The castle is great
there's no denying this and the arcades are unique"

Challenges imposed by writing poetry in dialect include engaging the reader with ease without the essence of subject matter being lost; carefully interpreting the sounds of an accent in ways that reflect its tones and nuances authentically, bearing in mind that this may differ according to the area (Cardiff accent varies across the city); the use of punctuation needs to be carefully considered —initially I over-used apostrophes as I thought that this would help the reader to decipher the content whereas it read better without them (diolch Mike Jenkins for guiding me through this).

Writing in dialect is rewarding in that the resulting poem feels real, true to the chosen area. It can add a level of humour which may be lacking in conventional styles and such poems are a joy to perform. The voice seems to add flavour. Expressions such as *inni luv, know whar I mean* and *i'll be there now in a minni* adds character and impact. It also gives the reader a chance to hear the dialect and even practice the accent should they wish. Ultimately having material written in this way means that local dialects are kept alive and in a country as linguistically diverse as Wales, what better reason could you want?

Inni luv

Like the caastle's great an all tha
no denyin an' the aarcades aar unique
Importan paart of our eritage and istory
I mean the Royal was built on slums demolished special
Not bein funny bu them families must've been gutted
Still...no lyin' it's dead pretty
Inni luv
An the maaarket's aardly changed
cept spaarks are massive now
ad a stall there originally like y'know
An the docks....sorry Bay
Well I never....very glam
An at leas the Ship's still open
Know whar I mean?
Bur I tells you wha
ang on a sec
aaarrigh luv?
Yeah on my way
I'll be there now in a minni
Sorry Drive...the ol man
Where was I to?
Yeah righ
Bes thing abou this place is the accent
I means i
I luuuvs tha' Caaardiff twang I doos
So lush
My mum ated i tho.

Delilah

Wassa marra wiv you?
S'only a song
I've nevva treated wimmin like tha
Nevva will
an I've bin singin this fur yers at the game
Jus as all me mates av
Wimmin too
S'tradition like
They should gerr on wiv sortin their ouse out
an lerr us carry on as if nuffin as appened
Ow aar we sposed t enjoy the rugby now?
S'ruined
Know warr I means?

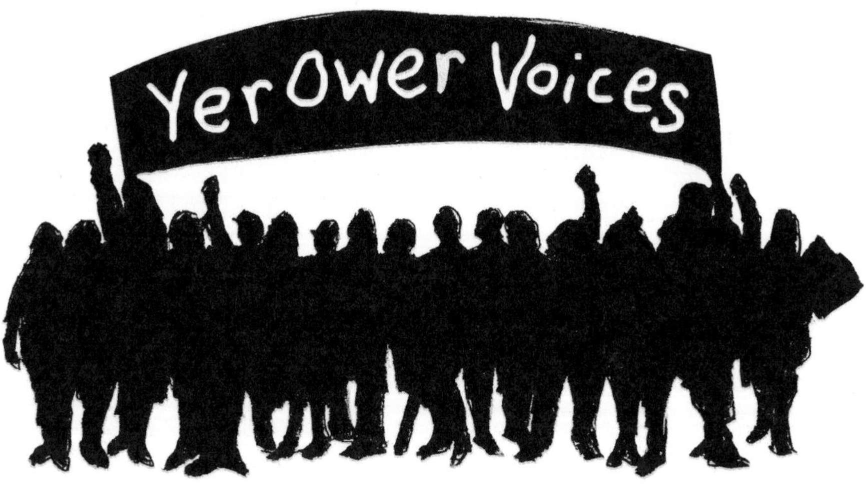

Pete Akinwunmi

As much as I love to write poems 'as they sound' I don't think it's necessary for every piece. I consider it as another feature of the 'artistry' of poetry to recognise when poems need the grit and reality of phonetics to illustrate the dialect. Often this requires deliberate misspelling even when it's unnecessary in order to relate what is being said to the manner of discourse of the poem's voice.

Having been brought up and lived in South Wales, my 'dialect voice' is naturally South Walian. The accent of Newport, my home town since 1980, is recognizably different to our nearest and largest neighbour, Cardiff. This is not easily conveyed in writing, although to the ear the difference in accent, dialect and word choice is often distinctive. Perhaps the most abiding challenge is to capture those individualisms of specific places so as to make them as recognizable in writing as they are to the ear.

I have considered writing in the voice of my family, which is English as spoken by Nigerians—this is a challenge that awaits me but which I have little doubt I will take on sometime. I haven't used the technique overmuch in my writing of poems although it has felt more natural when composing song lyrics. I'm aware this is perhaps a personal idiosyncrasy and would be pleased to discuss this further with other writers.

This Is Newport

This is Newport
where we're prowd t'live.
Nuthin t' lose ana bit less t'give.
These 'angin' streets,
which Chaahtists walked
ah where kids learn to fight
way before they can talk.
All these places we loves t'roam
The 'port en't much, but we calls it 'ome.

I could show you Cuhleon's bright spots where blads drive fast for fun;
or Pill's daark 'idin' places
where the 'babylon' never come.
Show you schools from 'Artridge to Dyffryn that stood and watched kids grow,
walk you through the streets of Ringlund
that taught them all they know...
Coz this is Newport where we're prowd t'live...

On top'f Twmbarlam's nipple,
dreamin' looking down
anundred an' fifty thousand dreamers struggle t'elp ah town.
Betrayed by the planners,
an' entrepreneurial flops
an' lazy-minded councillors who
emptied the streets of shops.
But it's still ah town
where we're prowd t'live...

Who said pride an'istory
count for bugger all?
I reckon John Frost-like heroics
can arrest this 'eadlong fall
inta the dust.
Coz there is a sense of inner strength,
a steel which forged its men.
Aye, the guts
that vanquished All Blacks
is stirrin' in the 'Port again.

When Jonny's TJ's lit a fuse
'cool Cymru' rocked ah town,
Dub War, Darlin' Buds, Feeder, the 'Dolls, Strummer and Cobain 'ung round.
A place of 'ard working people
and bangin' weekends in town—
cuz this is a place with edge and bite
not one that just lays down.

The 'port still as its icons
'Bomber' Pearce, and Benji's Skindred
Big Mac's soul; the Cowntee, the Dragons,
and a brand new maarkit
where the world can be fed!

Kenneth Baker and Paul Flynn;
as 'eroes not everyone's choice
but Newport caarvd these people,
as well as Harry Dibble—
and gave Frankie Lodge 'is voice.

We wuz once a town,
now promoted to 'city',
like big brother 'Diff down the road.
But up feels like down
when we drive out to Spytty
while the town centre corrodes.
But 'eld together it would seem
by expectant girls with pregnant dreams
who can drink the night and day away, dancin' from Le Pub to the Potter's and Meze.
Who drag their claahts through ugly and broke
into Newport men—ahrf tidy blokes.

The people of the 'port
are the lifeblood that it needs,
but they'll drain away
without a tourniquet
around the gash
the roads out of town leave.
There's pubs cold and empty,
town's wheezin' drawing breath;
p'rhaps walkin with the friars
is the first step to resurrect...

Ah Newport, where I'm prowd t'live...
with nothin' t'ide ana bit less to give.
For those whose lenses are uncorrupted
and are 'Port-people, life-long and uninterrupted,
will see that despite the chaos
thas erupted in recent times
there are loadsa optimistic souls
whose minds
an 'aarts are Newport dipped and yet remains.
So we have our shiny mall,
with toothy smiles and muzacked walls.
So we have a riverbank, where concrete grows
and to be frank, who knows
if they'll be lived
and loved like 'Pill' was and is?
Can our 'new' port stir the blood
of those who live and love in Bettws?
Will sharing a pint in the brand new Blaina Wharf hold more laughs or in any way be finer
than our ancient Murrenger?
Yes, McCann can fill the 'Blowa's shoes
and Le Pub will fill us with rock and blues. while new memories are forged.

For these are the streets,
where 'istory walks
an' where kids learn t'fight,
before they cn talk.
All these places
we loves to roam,
the 'port en't much,
but we calls it 'ome.

The Rugby Will Be Broadcast On the Television Shortly

Rugby's comin' on telly innit?
isson now in a minnitt.
Arf'narf done frarf time,
plenty uf Brain's an' a crate uf wine

Boys'll be ova now in a bit,
Dai'n 'iz brawd, 'oozas twp aza tit,
but keep 'im tidy an' he'll be fine
dippin' leeks in 'iz glass o'wine

"Wara teg, butt, shove up mun!"
I only went'check the curry's done
an Dai's brawd parked iz fat arse
in my bloody seat an' the game's gonna start!

They're comin out, they shut the roof,
they got bangerz'n sparklerz'n fire goin' off.
Don't give a toss for all that crap, mun;
"SHURRUP now twat, iss time for the anthem."

The boyz are all cwtchin now look,
hands on their arts
beltin' "Hen laid yn hadduck"
an' "Gwlad bloody Gwlad"

Can't hear a thing over ourselves,
drinkin'n linkin' an' singin' in Welsh.
I'm a patriot right, an' I know all the words
can't speak'm but still 'ope the old lingo endures (innit?)

Shoulda seen the place butt, after we scored,
arms in the air, Brains on the floor.
Ach-a-fi mind, the place is a tip
but full'f 'appy Taffies innit?

So after the game right, we ate all the grub
decanted then, down to the pub
where "Evans the Bread" stood a pint oniz ed
and sang 'Myfanwy'—in the key of Chubb!

We sang til we ached and laughed ourselves 'oarse
fedw gaib, an' still wantin' more.
10 o'clock an' Dai's brawd's in the loo
'finger-throatin' see, makin' more room!

I admit we left a bit of a mess,
a beer-mat got tore—an' I 'aff t'cunfess,
when I tipped that beer on the barmaid's vest
I didn' think she'd tell me to rub it in her chest!

6 Nation victors, Triple Crown or Grand Slam?
Plucky losers, wooden spoonists? Couldn't give a fukin' damn.
Duw Duw mun, iss always great
watchin' the match on the telly with all my mates.
(Innit?)

Iawn Cont?
—North & West Wales

Ifor Ap Glyn

Cefais fy magu ar aelwyd 'dwyieithog'—Mam yn siarad iaith Llanrwst a 'nhad yn siarad iaith y Cardi! Felly cefais gyflwyniad cynnar i'r amrywiaeth a'r cyfoeth sydd yn ein hiaith lafar, ond dylanwad mam fu gryfaf arnaf mae'n debyg, a'r ffaith 'mod i wedi byw ers 30 mlynedd yng ngweriniaeth y Cofi!

Er mai'r cywair llenyddol bydda'i'n ei ddefnyddio amlaf wrth ysgrifennu yn Gymraeg, dwi yn tueddu meddwl yn iaith Caernarfon a'r cylch. Felly, er imi ysgrifennu 'cadeiriau' dyweder, yr ynganiad 'cadeiria' fydd gen i yn fy mhen, a hynny o bosib yn odli hefo gair arall sy'n diweddu hefo '-a' mewn lein gyfagos. Bydda'i'n defnyddio geiriau mwy lleol hefyd, yn enwedig os ydynt yn cyfleu ystyr neu emosiwn yn well: sbybio, stid, sesbinio, ac y blaen—a dwi wedi arbrofi drwy ddefnyddio tafodieithoedd eraill ar gyfer ambell gerdd—iaith Aberteifi i gofio David Datblygu a'r Wenhwyseg i gofio plant Aberfan.

Mae tafodieithoedd newydd yn datblygu bellach, o gwmpas Caerdydd a'r ysgolion Cymraeg yn benodol, ac mae'r rheini'n dechrau darganfod eu lleisiau llenyddol eu hunain, sy'n beth braf—ond dwi'n gobeithio hefyd y bydd cyfoeth yr hen rai yn parhau i roi canllaw creadigol i'n awduron cyfoes. 'Yn y llafar, (nid mewn llyfr!) y mae ein lleufer'.

***

I was raised in a 'bilingual' home—Mam spoke Llanrwst Welsh and my Dad spoke Cardi! So, from an early age I was introduced to the dialectical variety and richness that exists in spoken Welsh; however, it was my mother's Gwynedd dialect that prevailed, reinforced by 30 years of living in the autonomous linguistic republic that is Caernarfon!

Although I use a fairly standard literary Welsh for most of my poems, I do tend to think in the dialect of the Caernarfon area. Accordingly, I might write 'cadeiriau', but I would definitely have the north-western pronunciation 'cadeiria' in mind and be looking to rhyme it with other words ending in '-a' in adjacent lines. Using dialect words appeals to me too, especially if they capture a particular meaning or emotion—words like sbybio, stid, sesbinio etc. I have experimented also with writing in other dialects of Welsh when appropriate—using some Aberteifi Welsh for a poem in memory of David Datblygu, and Gwenhwyseg or Glamorganshire Welsh in an elegy for the children of Aberfan.

These days there are new dialects of Welsh developing, particularly in Cardiff and the Welsh-medium schools of the south-east—and these are beginning to find their own literary voices, which is encouraging. However, I hope that the richness of some of the older dialects will continue to inform contemporary writing: 'yn y llafar, (nid mewn llyfr!) y mae ein lleufer'—'it's the spoken (not the written!) word that lights our way'.

Teach Yourself Cofi

Shrada Gymraeg cont;
duda rwbath 'dan ni'n ddallt.

Iawn bwoi:
deu-yd, gwneu-yd,
sgrin ia, niwc ia,
jiws buwch ia,
yr hen go, miglo, cae cicio,
stagio fodings ar 'Maes,
- paid galw bodan fi'n gacan!-
Sgubs, Maes Barcar,
Ysgol Maesincla;
c'laen 'ta.

Ond Cofis 'dan ni,
danim yn siarad
geiria Cymraeg mowr
fatha pobol Cymraeg iawn,
fatha pobol Dwyfor
ar y telifishyn.

'Arlwy'r sianel, etifeddiaeth y Cymro,
pesychwch fel y pesychasoch o'r blaen,
cynffon hefo Duw,
cerdd dant yn fyw,'

a tydi De Ffrainc
ddim yn Sowth o Ffrans,
iawn cont?
Iawn.

(*Atgynhychir y gerdd hon gyda chaniatâd Gwasg Carreg Gwalch*)

Teach Yourself Cofi

Speak to us in Welsh cont,
Say something we can understand...

Okay bwoy—
a sebra in a soo, yeah;
a nuke yeah, a screen too;
cow juice yeah;
sing the bell;
if you can't hear the smell on that
you must be blind;
don't moider me now, I'm all behind;
radi - Ator; hair- Dryer; corn - Flake;
eyeing up skirt on the Maes;
don't call my bird a cake!
Sgubs, Maes Barcar,
Ysgol Maesincla:
-let's be avin yah!

But we're Cofis, yeah?
We don' speak big Welsh words
like proper Welsh speakers,
like Pen Llŷn people on the telly:

‘A warming libation, soul of the nation,
with whom did you share
your hardwearing bloom?
St David’s Day rant; live cerdd dant’,

and our South of France’s not on the Med
but by the castle wall instead,
understood cont?
Understood.

(*translation by author*)

Notes to Teach Yourself Cofi

This poem began life as an attempt to translate Peter Finch’s performance piece, ‘A Guide to the Dialect’ into Welsh. Peter’s poem listed words to be read in a Cardiff accent, and I soon realised it would make more sense to write something similiar relating to Caernarfon. Twenty five years later, adapting ‘Teach Yourself Cofi’ back into English, I have adopted a similarly relaxed attitude to translation; it’s more of a ‘transcreation’, as Irish language poet Gabriel Rosenstock would put it!

Cofi (= covi)	Someone from Caernarfon who has a pronounced accent.
cont	Although it can be used in Caernarfon as it is in other parts of Wales with all the offensive force of its English counterpart, Cofis also use it more neutrally when talking to each other; like ‘mate’, both as greeting, and for emphasis: e.g. ‘they kept me there for an hour cont!’
sebra, soo	Cofis, like many in north west Wales, have difficulty in differentiating between s and z in English. (There is no z sound in Welsh)

nuke	(niwc) a penny.
screen	(sgrin) a pound.
sing the bell, hear the smell	translations from Welsh idiom.
radi-Ator etc	putting the emphasis on the penultimate syllable is a characteristic of the Welsh language—some pronounce English words in the same way.
Maes	the square in the middle of town.
Sgubs	(Lôn Ysgubor Goch) a main road on one of the town's council estates, as is Maes Barcar.
proper Welsh	Wherever you go in Wales, everyone thinks someone somewhere else speaks better Welsh than they do—an inferiority complex that you never encounter amongst English speakers. Sadly Caernarfon is no exception.

Ness Owen

Working in a F.E. college in a bilingual community for many years, where dialects and languages naturally mix, has always been a delight and fascination for me. Growing up on the most westerly side of Ynys Mon, an island off the north coast, I was always aware of the mixing of Welsh and English in some people's natural speech. I was also aware of the tendency to apologise for the language *ability* or the lack of it: I have often heard the phrase: *'Sorry, I only speak Holyhead Welsh'* as if it wasn't quite good enough or perhaps somewhere along the line they had been told that it was wrong.

This flies against the fact that to be able to code switch between languages or borrow from other languages is actually a gift from our environment and connected to place. Though I have been guilty of language apology myself many times, I wanted to write a poem that challenges this apology and hopefully celebrates what is ours to share.

Wyt ti'n siarad Gymraeg?

(For M)

Fedra i ddim,'sdi*

Not proper Cymraeg
not like the cloman drws nesa
sbio-lawr-ei-thrwyn-a-busnesa**
sayin' I'm not a real Cymro and
those teachers from the mountains
still in my head sayin' chwara teg
for tryin', but Holyhead-Welsh
won't get you far.

Cwilidd o beth***
hurts my heart if I'm honest.
Shouldn't 'ave sat at the back
at ysgol Sul. Mam's fault

keepin' it from me, only
speakin' it when she was
rhempio or janglin' with
Pero y ci.

This is me with half my
tongue. Too old to be changin'
'cept sometimes at the bottom
of a glass, in a burgundied corner
of the Branch, they flow out from
somewhere, these words I've
been chasin' all my life.
Iawn, hogia. Croeso 'nôl!

Notes —
*I can't, you know
**Daft woman next door/ looking down her nose and noseying
***An embarrassment
Ysgol Sul --- Sunday school
Rhempio — ranting
Pero y ci — Pero the dog
Iawn, hogia. Croeso 'nôl! — Ok, lads. Welcome back.

Gwenno Gwilym

I ddechra fo, dwi'n sgwennu mewn tafodiaith achos ma'n dipyn o laff. Dwi'n lyfio adio -io i verbs Saesneg a gneud iddyn nw odli efo geiria Cymraeg a ma sgwennu geiria Seasneg yn Gymraeg yn ffyni.

Hefyd, dwi'n meddwl fod o'n bwysig cael representation realistic o sut da ni'n siarad ar bapur. Tyda ni ddim yn siarad mewn Cymraeg perffaith drw'r adag, nadan? Felly does dim rhaid sgwennu fel na drw'r adag, nagoes?

Dwi'n licio chopïo, mixio a innovatio. Dwi'n mwynhau cadw list o'r holl direct translations dwi'n dod ar draws o ddydd i ddydd, dwi'n ffindio nw'n fascinating a ma'n cracio fi fyny.

Dwi'm isio mynd lawr y route political pan dwi'n trafod y peth achos dwi'm yn neud o i fod yn political. Dwi'n neud o i fod yn ddoniol, authentic ac accessible. (Ma hynna braidd yn political wan, dydi?) Eniwê...dwi'n meddwl yn y bôn, dwi just yn chwara a trio tynnu llun efo geiria achos dyna di barddoniaeth, de?

***

To start with, I write in dialect because it's a bit of a laff. I love adding -io to English verbs and making them rhyme with Welsh words and writing English words in Welsh is ffyni.

Also, I think it's important to have a realistic representation of how we speak on paper. We don't always speak in perfect Welsh, do we? So, we don't always have to write like that, do we?

I like to chopïo, mixio and innovatio. I enjoy keeping a list of all the direct translations I come across in everyday life, I find them fascinating, and they crack me up.

I don't want to go down the political route when I'm discussing this because I'm not doing it to be political. I'm doing it to be entertaining, authentic and accessible. (Although, that statement is a bit political, isn't it?). Anyway.... I think that, in the bone, I'm just playing and trying to pull a picture with words because that's what poetry is, isn't it?

Y Gymraes yma

Ella fod y ~~Cymraes~~ Gymraes yma
ddim bob tro yn treiglo
a di byth yn mynd i Steddfod
a does gan y Gymraes yma ddim
gradd da yn y Gymraeg
(Ond mai'n hoffi ~~quotio~~ dyfynnu caneuon Datblygu)
ag yn ~~amal aml~~ amal (?) ma'r Gymraes yma yn gorfod
llenwi ffurflenni yn Saesneg
ac angen ~~mam~~ ei mham i gywiro
ei ~~cerddi~~ cherddi

Ac er fod y Gymraes yma yn byw
~~miles~~ filltiroedd o adra
ag ar adega yn anghofio'r gair cywir
yn ei iaith gynta
dydi'r Gymraes yma byth yn bell o'i
gwreiddia
achos ma'i chartref yn byw yn
ei geiria

~~Y Gymraes yma~~ This Welsh Lady

Maybe she doesn't always ~~treiglo~~ mutate
and she never goes to the Eisteddfod
and she doesn't have a
~~gradd da yn y Gymraeg~~ good degree in Welsh
(but she likes to ~~dyfynnu~~ quote Datblygu)
~~Yn amal aml amal (?)~~ Most of the time she has to
fill forms in ~~Saesneg~~ English
and still needs her ~~Mam~~ Mum
to proofread her poems

Even though she lives
~~milltiroedd~~ miles from ~~adra~~ home
and at times can't think of the word
in her ~~iaith gynta~~ first language
she is never far from her
~~gwreiddia~~ roots
because her home lives
in her ~~geiria~~ words

Paid â siarad Lobsgows

Main ingredients yn cynnwys
Mam Gymraeg ag English father
Ysgol Dyffryn Conwy a Coleg lawr coast
Wedyn bach o verbs wedi'i cymysgu efo io's
chopïo, mixio, innovatio
Chwysu'r treigladau caled i neud nw'n soft
Gadael iddo ffrwtian drwy gydol dy arddegau
mutatio, adaptio, anghofio
Pinsh o direct translations
(Neith Mam dy dynnu di fyny ar hynny most likely)
Llond llaw o embarrassment a peer pressure i addurno
Gweini gyda side order o reality
Enjoy

Don't speak Lobscouse

Main ingredients include
Welsh Mam and English Dad
Ysgol Dyffryn Conwy and Coleg down the coast
Add a few verbs mixed with io's
chopïo, mixio, innovatio
Sweat the mutations until they are soft
Simmer throughout your adolescence
mutatio, adaptio, forgetio
A pinch of direct translations
(Mam will pull you up on that one most likely)
Handful of embarrassment and peer pressure to decorate
Serve with a side order of reality
Enjoy

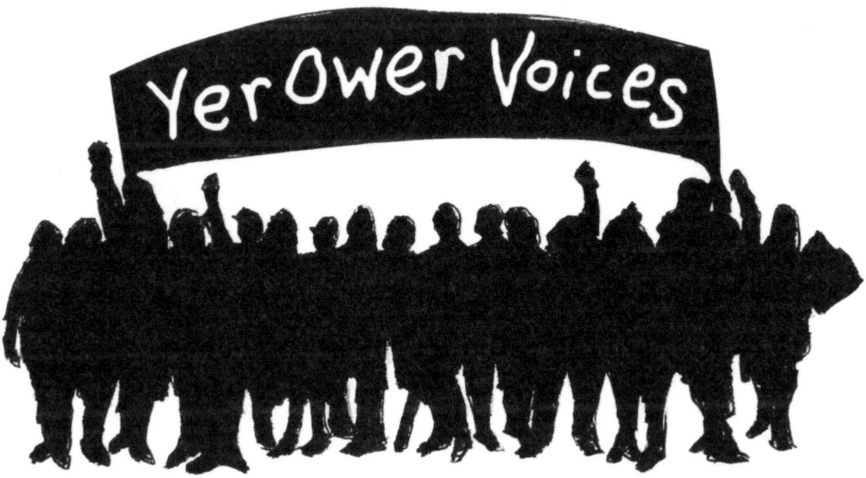

Sara Louise Wheeler

My father's family hail from the village of Rhosllannerchrugog, a coal-mining district in North-East Wales. The coal-rich land attracted people from all over Wales and beyond, resulting in a thriving industry and associated community. A plethora of Welsh dialects developed, whilst non-Welsh speakers quickly learnt the language. This melting pot of inhabitants were engaged daily in translanguaging whilst communicating.

Consequently, a distinctive and esoteric dialect of Welsh emerged, reflecting the main local industry and the linguistic diversity drawn upon; words such as 'beindin', to mean 'a little bit extra', came from the extra rock left on the roof when cutting passages, to avoid the collapsing of the tunnels.

I was raised in a bilingual household, speaking my paternal family's dialectical Welsh. My mother attended night classes to learn Welsh, and I recall a fascinating discussion over dinner one evening, where she recounted her tutor's assertion that some of the words she had learnt from my father were, in fact, 'not words'. Additionally, Alwen, my paternal grandmother, and her sister, Gwladys, often said that their dialectical Rhos Welsh was 'not correct Welsh'. In the secondary school I attended in Wrexham, it has historically been noted, including in an academic text about dialects, that Rhos Welsh was the subject of negative prestige by teachers and pupils—this is something I can attest to.

I have always, therefore, been fascinated by dialects, particularly my own, and I have studied them in a variety of mediums, as an academic and through my creative writing. I write the column *''O'r gororau'* in *Barddas* Welsh poetry magazine, and the editor, Twm Morys, has always supported my dialectical writing, including publishing the poem in this collection, which is a homage to Rhos dialect. Despite criticisms and derision relating to my dialect, I have also been inspired by the works of Benjamin Zephaniah, Patience Agbabi, Aled Lewis Evans, Dennis Potter, Anthony Burgess, David Mitchell, Daniel Lloyd, Rufus Mufasa and Bethany Handley.

I feel that dialect writing is an important part of my own journey of self-discovery, and the preservation and celebration of a dialect which has been such an important part of my identity and that of my family and community. It seems to me that this is a common feeling for writers all over the world, and that this is a theme which brings us together and can help us to understand each other through shared experiences.

Dio'm yn Gymraeg iawn, chwaith

(Teyrnged i Nain ac Anti Gwladys)

Mae nene'n naci tydi? Lle ges ti fe? O ene, ia?
Ti'n edrych yn *bropor* ynddo fe cofia. Ni 'di bod yn 'sidro
mynd ene, i brynu 'chydig o bethe—mae'r lle 'ma fatha
pontecel! Ond dene fo, ynde, sdim ishio sbonclo nagoes,
mae'r pres yn mynd fel y *gynjar* i ninlle, dyddiau 'ma.

Dere mewn i'r tŷ rŵan, neu byddi ti'n *starfio* siŵr—be?
Naci, naci, dyna ein gair ni—am fod yn rhy oer, ia, ia,
dim byd i wneud hefo bwyd na na; dwi'm yn siŵr
pam ni'n dweud nene yma, Cymraeg y Rhos ynde, ond dene fo—
dio'm yn Gymraeg iawn nadi, ond dene sut ni wastad 'di siarad,
yma'n y pentref ar y mynydd.

Ew roedd hi'n grêt yma ers talwm, cofia—mynd i'r eglwys,
a cherdded yn dôl lawr y lôn, a phawb wrthi'n
canu a siarad. Doedd gennym ni ddim llawer cofia, a finnau yn
byw ar bron i ddim byd—byth yn bwyta, ac eto
wnes i erioed ddal dim byd naddo—ges i ddim y *dip*,
a phawb arall yn sâl hefo fo. Oedd, roedden nhw'n ddyddiau da.

Ges i *job* mewn swyddfa unwaith, a'r bos o'r De 'cw yn rhywle,
a fo'n siarad hefo fi, a finnau yn gor'od d'eud wrtho 'dwi'n rili sori,
ond wnei di siarad yn Saesneg i ni gael deall ein gilydd?' Cywilydd,
yndê, ond dene fo chi'n gweld—Cymraeg Rhos, dio'm yn
Gymraeg iawn, nadi?

Hei, es i draw i weld Beti diwrnod o'r blaen,
a hithau 'di cael carped newydd—ew, mae hi 'di gneidi, siŵr—
yn cael pawb draw i'r tŷ i gael sbec arno.

Wyt ti moyn bwyd, cariad? Fedra'i wneud pastai grochan
ac mae 'na *corn beef* ene, os ti'n licio'w? Ac wedyn pastai fale,
a gei di dop y llefrith arni, os tishio'w?

Dene fo yndê, ond paid â gadael i ni dy fwydro di—
cadwa di fyny yn dysgu Cymraeg iawn yn yr ysgol—
tydi Cymraeg ni ddim gwerth nadi?
Dio'm yn Gymraeg iawn chwaith—well i ti beidio pigo fo fyny—
dio'm yn iawn, nadi, ddim yn Gymraeg iawn chwaith.

Rhosllannerchrugog yn yr wythdegau/ Cilgwri 2020

It's not proper Welsh, either

(A tribute to my grandmother and Great Aunty Gwladys)

That's naci isn't it? Where did you get it? Oh there yes?
You look proper in it see. We've been thinking
of going there, to buy a few things—this place is like
pontecel! But there we are, there's no need to sbonclo is there,
money goes like the gynjar to nowehere, these days.

Come into the house now, or you'll be starving indeed—what?
No, no, that's our word—for being cold, yes, yes,
nothing to do with food no, no; I'm not sure
why we say that here, it's Rhos Welsh, but there we are,
it's not proper Welsh is it, but that's how we've always spoken,
here in the village on the mountain.

Oh it was great here in the old days, you know—going to church,
and walking back down the lane, and everyone would be
singing and talking. We didn't have much you know, and I
lived on next to nothing—didn't eat, and yet
I never caught anything did I—I never got the *dip*,
and everyone else was sick with it. Oh yes, they were good days.

I got a job in an office once, and the boss was from the south somewhere,
and he spoke to me, and I had to say 'I'm really sorry,
but could you speak in English so we can understand each other?'
Oh, the shame isn't it, but there we are you see—
Rhos Welsh, it isn't proper Welsh, is it?

Hey, I went over to see Beti the other day,
she's had a new carpet—oh, she's made up with it sure,
having everyone over to look at it.

Do you want some food, cariad? I can make hash
and there's corn beef there, if you like it? And then apple pie,
and you can have the top of the milk on it, if you want it?

There we are, isn't it, but don't let us confuse you,
keep going with your learning proper Welsh in school,
our Welsh is no good is it? It's not proper Welsh either,
you'd best not pick it up;
It's not right, is it, not proper Welsh either.

Note — Rhosllannerchrugog in the eighties/ Wirral 2020

Aled Lewis Evans

Pan oeddwn yn athro mewn ysgol uwchradd Cymraeg yn Wrecsam am dros ddegawd, fe wnes i ddod ar draws tafodiaith a oedd yn gymysg o'r Gymraeg a ddysgwyd yn bennaf drwy addysg, a Saesneg y Gogledd Ddwyrain.

Roedd rhai o'r cyfuniadau o'r ddwy iaith yn ddoniol, ond weithiau hefyd yn naturiol i'r siaradwyr.

Mae canran uchel o fyfyrwyr addysg uwchradd wedi dysgu'r Gymraeg yn yr ysgolion cynradd, ac yna yn parhau efo'u haddysg ac yn adlewyrchu cymysgedd o'r ddwy iaith ar brydiau. Roedd yn amlwg fod y termau addysgol yn Gymraeg ond yna'r Saesneg yn ei glymu efo'i gilydd.

Roedd eithriadau i hyn wrth gwrs, a rhai o'r bobl hyn o'u cyfarfod fel oedolion wedi siarad Cymraeg cywirach, neu wedi "colli" y Gymraeg, nid yn arddel mwyach y Wenglish sydd yn gyfaddawd rywsut rhwng y ddau. Roedd dealltwriaeth y disgyblion o'r Gymraeg yn dda, ac efallai roedd elfen o ddiogi, a diffyg cyfleoedd i siarad yn y cyfnod hwnnw.

Ond ar y pryd fel athro ifanc dechreuais weld yr hiwmor yn y sefyllfaoedd hyn oherwydd y cyfuniadau iaith. Y gerdd fwyaf poblogaidd o safbwynt hyn oedd 'Over The Llestri' a nifer yn medru uniaethu efo'r sefyllfaoedd a'r termau. Wrth gwrs maen nhw yn adlewyrchu cyfnod arbennig, ond mae'r ddealltwriaeth yn dal yno, er gwaethaf y newid termau. Pan oeddwn yn darllen y gerdd mewn darlleniadau roedd yn cael derbyniad da fel arfer. Rwy'n cofio ei ddarllen unwaith mewn ardal Gymreig iawn a doedd yr ymateb yn hollol groes i hynny—efallai oherwydd bod y gynulleidfa yn meddwl mod i yn dibrisio'r Gymraeg. Ond un eithriad oedd hwn. I mi roedd yn nodwedd o ffin y gogledd—ddwyrain yn yr 1990au, ond teg dweud bod Wenglish yn dafodiaith mewn mannau eraill hefyd.

Mae'r gerdd 'Chwedlau' yn codi o sefyllfa lle roedd disgyblion yn trafod chwedl enwog Llyn y Fan mewn ieithwedd oedd yn adlewyrchu mwy ar eu byd a'u rhagdybiaethau hwy. Yna'r athro yn sôn y bydd yn symud ymlaen at chwedl Macsen Wledig yr wythnos ganlynol. Mae ychydig o ddeialog, rhwng disgybl ac athro sydd yn ddigon ysgafn—a'r athro yn cyfaddawdu rhywfaint drwy ymateb mewn ieithwedd debyg yn ôl. Dipyn o hiwmor eto oedd y nod. Mae cyfeirio at gyfnod pan oedd Pamela Anderson yn seren *Baywatch*. Mae'r gerdd o bosibl yn gynnyrch ei gyfnod sef yr 1990au, ac efallai wrth ysgrifennu rŵan y byddai rhywun yn fwy gofalus yn ei gyfeiriadaeth. Ond ysgrifennu oeddwn ar gyfer oedolion yn y bôn—rhai mae'n siŵr yn gwaredu at dafodiaith o'r fath. Ond yr unig nod i mi oedd hiwmor y sefyllfaoedd, a'r asio ar ddau fyd—a Chymraeg safonol yn cwrdd â Saesneg y stryd.

***

When I was a teacher in a Welsh secondary school in Wrexham for over a decade, I encountered a dialect that was a mixture of the Welsh that was learned mainly through education, and the English of North East Wales. Some of the combinations of the two languages were funny, but also sometimes natural for the speakers.

A high percentage of secondary education students have learned Welsh in primary schools, and then continue with their education and reflect a mixture of both languages at times. It was clear that the educational terms were in Welsh, but then the English tied it together.

There were exceptions to this of course, and some of these people when I met them as adults had spoken more correct Welsh, or had "lost" the Welsh, no longer engaging with the Wenglish dialect which is somehow a compromise between the two. The pupils' understanding of the Welsh language was good, and perhaps there was an element of laziness, and a lack of opportunities to speak Welsh outside school in that period.

But at the time as a young teacher, I started to see the humour in these situations because of the language combinations. The most popular poem from this point of view was 'Over the Llestri' and many could identify with the situations and the educational terms of the time. Of course, they reflect a certain period, but the understanding is still there, despite the change of terms. When I read the poem in readings it was usually well received. I remember, however, reading it once in a very Welsh area and the reaction was completely the opposite—perhaps because the audience thought I was devaluing the Welsh language, and making fun of something that was too close for comfort. But this was one exception. For me it was a feature of the north-east borderland in the 1990s, but it's fair to say that Wenglish is a dialect in other places too.

The poem 'Chwedlau' arises from a situation where pupils were discussing the famous tale of Llyn y Fan in a language that reflected more on their world and their assumptions. Then the teacher mentions that he will move on to the legend of Macsen Wledig the following week. There is a bit of dialogue, between pupil and teacher which is light enough—and the teacher compromises somewhat by responding in similar language back. A bit of humour again was the goal. It refers to a time when Pamela Anderson was the star of *Baywatch*. The poem is possibly a product of its time, the 1990s, and perhaps when writing now someone would be more 'careful' regarding this. But I certainly enjoyed the children's openness. I was basically writing for adults—and some readers perhaps would have been challenged by seeing this in print. But the only aim for me was to reflect the humor of the situations, and the blending of two worlds—standard Welsh meets border English speak.

Chwedlau

"That Morwyn Llyn y Fan
was dead tight on him.
Dead shady. I'd 'ave biffed her one.
Wnaeth o ddim ond cyffwrdd hi tair gwaith *like"*

Wythnos nesa mi fyddwn ni'n darllen
Chwedl Macsen Wledig.

"Oh ay, and who's he when he's at home?
Is he 'ard? does he live down Queen's Park?"

Yndi Daryl,
mae o'n *dead 'ard.*
Enw'i gariad o ydy Pamela Anderson,
ac maen nhw'n byw yng Nghaernarfon.

"Dwi'n gutted.
Roeddwn i wastad yn meddwl fod Pammy yn cariad fi *like..."*

Over the Llestri

Haia, has the gloch gone?
My dosbarth cofrestru's got
gwasanaeth this morning.
I don't bother with the llyfr emynau anymore
They put all the emynau on the Sgrin Rhyngweithiol.

I've got to go to the Mynedfa Disgyblion anyway
to fill a ffurflen hwyr.
Don't see the point
cause I'm 'Yma' now.
I preferred goin' to the Swyddfa,
but that's a parth di-blant now.
I hope they don't call me on the tanwydd, or e mail me mam
cause I wanted to wag Bacc Cymraeg in the bog, or the Llyfrgell.

What are you doin' for your Gweithgareddau?
Aps Cymraeg or Garddio?
I did Blodau Sych last year.
Have you paid your blaendal for the gwibdaith?
I've forgotten my ffurflen ganiatâd and my ffurflen B,
but I'm going to Zip World
cos it beats Castell Harlech any day.

Have you done your gwaith cartref in Gwyddoniaeth
on the mwynau?
Can I see your taflen cofnodi
and copio fyny the gwaith dosbarth and the arbrawf?
What was your Canlyniadau?

And don't mention Hanes. I hate Hanes!
We'll probably have to do sbwriela
around the Cae Bob Tywydd
and the cabanau for a whole tymor.
I'm sick of sbwriela!

What did you get in your prawf barddoniaeth?
Well she can't breathe on me
cause I've done my Gwerthfawrogiad on the Smotyn,
I've learnt what an englyn is,
how many sills its got and that,
and I've even watched "Traed mewn Cyffion"
I'd be dead good at Cymraeg
if the treigladau weren't there.
They should be scrapped.
Treiglad trwyn or something
it really does me 'ead in!

Hey, she's been a right slebog that Madonna when she was young,
She brought out a book once called "Rhyw".

Have you done all your gwaith cwrs then?
We've got the arholiad llafar soon.
She wants to siarad un wrth un with me
this arholwr about my diddordebau.
What's your Diddordebau?
I'm gonna say "Rhyw" like Madonna.
Hey if I said that for my Cyflwyno Gwybodaeth
I'd have to take the arholwr to the Stafell Feddygol
for a gorffwys.

Are you staying on for Blwyddyn deuddeg?
There's loads of gwersi rhydd.
Where are you goin on your Profiad Gwaith?

Well, they're sending me to some Swyddfa
where I'll have to be rhyngweithiol on the cyfrifiaduron,
and dwyieithog, and do some kind of cyflwyniad when I get back.
And it's getting me down already,
cause as you know,
I never speak a word of Welsh!

Maggie Harris

I am a Guyanese writer living in the UK, and lived in Wales between 2006-2017. Twice winner of The Guyana Prize for Poetry, the Caribbean Winner of the Commonwealth Short Story Prize and the 2020 Winner of the Wales Poetry Award, I have written 10 books. My latest short story collection is *Writing on Water* (Seren Books), and latest poetry book is *On Watching a Lemon Sail the Sea* (Cane Arrow Press). A new poetry collection, *I Sing with the Greenhearts*, will be published by Seren in 2025.

I write in both Standard English and Guyanese Creole. There have been many conversations around the authenticity of an oral language being recognised as more than dialect and as a language in its own right. The unique history of the Caribbean was founded on slavery, which displaced tribal African peoples, forcing them onto plantations, separating them from family groups and languages.

Languages that developed from enslavement would include Dutch, French, English and English idioms, added to traces of their original mother tongues. Poets like Louise Bennett (Miss Lou), Michael Smith (Jamaica), and Kamau Brathwaite, (Barbados, also a historian), would challenge the empirical status of the English language as not being representative of modern Caribbean peoples, and used their poetry to question and create a political and artistic space to reclaim an African identity—and for Creole, which Brathwaite described as Nation Language, to be recognised as a language.

My early attempts at writing Creole came up against the problem of writing a landscape poem in an oral tongue, as my learning of pastoral poetry was used to Wordsworth and his contemporaries. There was a fair amount of exploration that led to me producing the text, in an early poem called 'The Limbo Walkers'. Examples of Creole poetry would vary from island to island, and Guyana, the only English-speaking country in South America. My poem 'Cwmpengraig, Place of Stones', carries the tension of Welsh and English in its title; set in both geographical and historic locations, my presence in a Welsh valley with a working mill, acknowledges the journey of Welsh migration to South America.

The poem cried out for a three-layered representation through language, without which, the whole story couldn't be told. The nature of rivers is an apt metaphor for journeyers, a life force that is spiritual, fluid, and transformative.

Having the gift of Menna Elfyn's translation is vital; there really are three languages in this poem. When spoken, the poem takes on another layer, of voice and pronunciation.

An early reading of this poem was filmed at Borth, (on YouTube) with Vahni Capildeo. What may not be visibly present in the poem however, is the knowledge of Menna's familiarity with Cwmpengraig; her grandfather is buried in the cemetery up the hill. Welsh speakers may be able to pick this up through reading Menna's version, similarly to Guyanese readers who may find details that particularly singularises their intimacy of place and language, e.g. the opening lines, 'where yuh navel string bury is not necessarily home.'

Cwmpengraig, Place of Stones

Where yuh navel string bury is not necessarily home
Dis gurl gon walk my grandmother said
And walk I walk from Guyana to West Wales
And leave I leave that place of oceans and slave bones
For bruk down cottages and hills where people still pray

And come I come with my forked tongue split syntax
Of Hinglish and street Creole to wander lanes
With no names and no map where even
Sat-nav wuk hard to find being alimbo
Beyond satellite beyond stars

And stars and dreams of stars and songs
Called these Welsh from home
To cross oceans to a continent
Of the imagination

And is peel dis country peel like onions
Garden cups my cottage in its fists of seasons
Caring nothing for my ignorance
Of names, pronunciation, language

And History running in the stream right there
Beneath the stone: mill worker foot-bottom still indent
Ghost voice talking story wild a catchafire
How he catching boat with intention get the hell outa dis place

It nat fuh he to know some gurl would bring his story
Right back here and tell him tales of sugarcane
And captains tracing latitude and longitude
With quadrant, quill and octopus ink

Is laugh he would laugh true true
Whilst that stream keep gurgling
Stones keep tumbling
Underscore the footfall of my feet

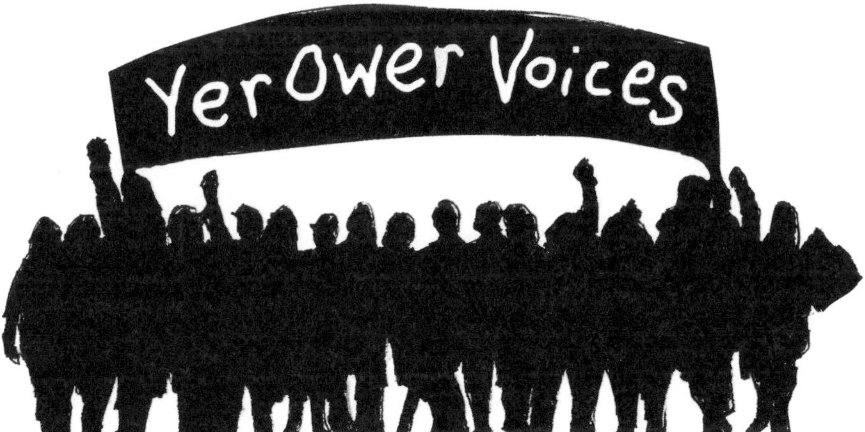

Menna Elfyn

Gofynnodd Maggie Harris i mi gyfieithu ei cherdd am Gwmpengraig ac roeddwn yn hapus i wneud gan fod teulu fy nhad o Drefach Felindre a'r capel Soar yng Nghwmpengraig lle byddwn yn treulio fy hafau ar wyliau gyda dad-cu a mam-gu Deri yn y chwedegau. Roedd cael naws newydd y lle drwy eiriau Maggie yn hyfryd i'w trosi.

Maggie Harris asked me to translate her poem 'Cwmpengraig' and I was happy to do so because my father's family are from Trefach Velindre and Capel Soar in Cwmpengraig, a place where I spent my summers and holidays with my grandparents in the 60s. Maggie provides a fascinating new insight into the place and it was a pleasure to translate.

Cwmpengraig

Nage lle mae'ch llinyn bogail wedi ei gladdu
Yw'ch cartre—mae'r groten ma'n mynd i fynd yn bell
A mynd yn bell wnes i o Guyana i Orllewin Cymru,
Gadel, gadel y lle oedd yn llawn esgyrn caethweision
A moroedd. A chael yn ei le, adfeilion o fythynnod a bryniau
Lle mae rhai yn dal i weddïo.

A dod gyda ' nhafod , dwy fforch iddi, ffordd o siarad hollt
Rhyw lediaith o Saesneg a Chreoleg y strydoedd, i grwydro
Lonydd heb enwau na map a lle mae hyd yn oed Sat-Nav
Yn gwegian ar goll, mewn gwagle
Heibio i'r lloeren , heibio i'r sêr.

A sêr a breuddwydion am sêr ac alawon
Wedi ei henwi'n yr heniaith, oddi cartre
I groesi o gefnfor i gyfandir
Y dychymyg.

Ac yn pilo'r wlad, ei bilo fel winwns
Llond dysgl o ardd yn ei ddyrnau o dymhorau,
Gan boeni'r iot am fy anwybodaeth
Am enwau, ynganu, iaith na hanes
Sy'n llifo o'r nant honco monco
Ger y garreg; ôl troed a gwadn gweithiwr
O'r felin yno o hyd, a llais ysbryd yn gof
Y cyfarwydd am y goelcerth
Fel y daliodd gwch gyda'r bwriad o sgathru
A baglu hi o'r lle. A phwy feddylie y bydde rhyw ferch
Yn dod â'r stori nol yn ei chôl gan sôn am blanhigion siwgr
A chapteniaid fyddai'n olrhain lledred a hydred
Cwadrant y lle, gyda chwilsyn ac inc otopws.

Am chwerthin—fydde'n marw o chwerthin,
Ar fy myw tra bydd y nant yn barbalu
A cherrrig yn dymchwel,
Dan fy nhraed, dan droedle fy nhraed.

Cyf:o'r Saesneg gan Menna Elfyn

Jacqueline Jones

I write in West Wales Pembrokeshire dialect. Some of the words migrated to South Wales during times of industry and are still spoken today. Most of what begins as slang or Urban speak eventually finds its way into the mainstream. I have been influenced by a lot of anthologies of Scots writing, some of it in Lallans.

A lot of writing to gets cast aside as parochial when it is part of the greater evolving fabric, the melting pot of migration. Creating works that evolve out of this diversity is one reward. The difficulty is the challenge, and this is endless. The words reflect the Viking, Flemish, Norman, Irish and English influences in Pembrokeshire—for example *hagglestone* (hailstone), a *bittie balshag* (ragged person).

As dialect is transported new words and identities are created ie lobscawsen became Scouser. A bit of meat or cheese served with cawl derived from North Walians escaping poverty in the Port of Liverpool. This is a fine example of Welsh rural dialect becoming part of the city, and forming a new identity.

To The Bar

She all to clush
Allfront
Eyes like babaloobies
A bittie balshag
But really cackty
Cack handed Cadge
Chopsy too
Taking the capswabble
A bit of a drapsy dolie
They say, a dimp
She no dj, but funkin
On a tammat
And cold as a hagglestone
But all a beleejers
At the Bar.

And furren
When the jar is bare
She will bellow like a wild horse
Tamping down the drang.

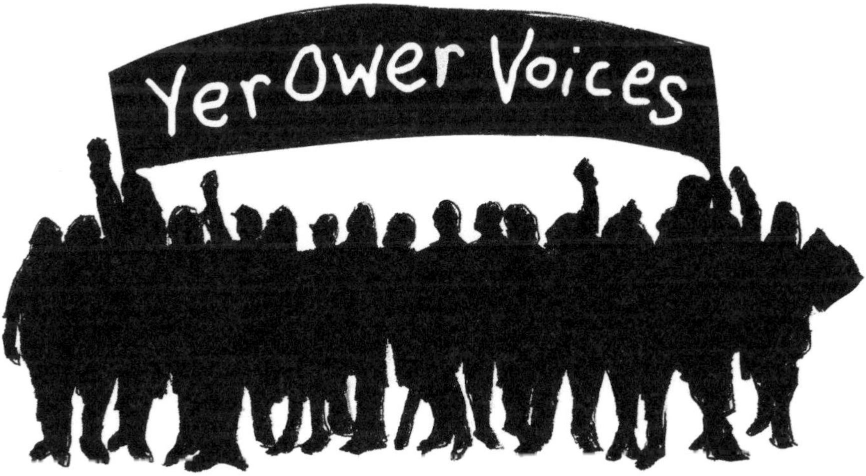

Acknowledgements

David Hughes	'Bigan Brave' — *Poetry Wales* 1998 'Prof' — *Poetry Wales* 2020 'On My Life—Tidy Boy', Swansea Poetry Workshop 1998 'Like Rome, Like' — *Working Out*, Parthian 2021 'Livin' — *Working Out*, Parthian 2021.
Stephen Knight	'At the Foot of Division Four', 'The Heart of Saturday Night' and 'Port Talbot' — *The Sandfields Baudelaire* (smiths|doorstop, 1996). 'A Swansea Adolescence', 'In This Dream of Swansea' — *A Swansea Love Song* (smith|doorstop, 2017).
Gemma June Howell	'Benefit Fraud' & 'Another Bun in the Oven' — *Red Poets* 'Rock Life' — *17 Poems from the Welsh Valleys* (MYscellaneoUS Press, 2015). 'Another Bun in the Oven' was in *Hallelujah for 50ft Women* (Bloodaxe Books, 2015) 'Another Bun in the Oven' and 'Benefit Fraud' was in *Ymlaen!/Onward*, Culture Matters.
Mike Jenkins	'Igh Sheriff of Merthyr' — *Red Poets* & title poem of next collection in dialect (published by Carreg Gwalch) *Ey Mister Lan'lor'* — www.culturematters.org.uk.
Kitty Jay	'Wossa Point Mun?' written by Julie K Watkins @ Kitty Jay 2023.
Tôpher Mills	'A Child's Christmas in Cardiff' was in *Cabaret 246* 'Nevuh Fuhget Yuh Kaairdiff' was in *Poetry Wales* Both in *The Bicycle is an Easy Pancake* (Red Sharks Press) 'Buying Shares in the Jobcentre' was in *Red Poets* 'Angin About' was in *Gwerfyl/Uprising*, and both *The Dancing Drayman* (Red Sharks Press)

'The Last Drunk In The Pub' was in *The Yellow Crane*, and is from *Swimming In The Living Room* (Red Sharks Press). 'Reemaaaarrkaabul' is from *Sex On Toast* (Parthian). 'Kaairdiff Maarket' was published in *Duke Street Arcade* by Cardiff: City Of Arcades. Uncollected.

Peter Finch

'Kerdif' and 'Partisan' appear in *Collected Poems* (Seren). Kerdif is also engraved on the entrance glass to Cardiff's main Hayes Library.

lloyd robson

'letter from sissi' (an extract) — *letter from sissi* (black hat, 1997)
'punchin out tha lights' — *edge territory* (black hat, 1996)
'words undeserving' — BBC Radio 4, 2021
'a curious pace' (an extract) — *The Big Book of Cardiff* (Seren, 2005).

Gwenno Gwilym

'Y Gymraes Yma'
Cyhoeddwyd 'Y Gymraes Yma' yn wreiddiol yng Nghyfrol Gwyl y Ferch 2022.
'Y Gymraes Yma' was originally published in *Cyfrol Gwyl y Ferch* 2022.
'Paid â siarad Lobsgows'
Cyhoeddwyd 'Paid â siarad Lobsgows' yn wreiddiol yn *Ffosfforws, Rhifyn 1, Cyhoeddiadau'r Stamp*, 2021
'Paid â siarad Lobsgows' was originally published in *Ffosfforws — Rhifyn 1, Cyhoeddiadau'r Stamp*, 2021.

Sara Louise Wheeler

'Dio'm yn Gymraeg iawn, chwaith' published in *Barddas*, Rhifyn Haf 2020.

* 9 7 8 1 9 1 2 7 1 0 5 4 6 *
BV - #0062 - 250823 - C0 - 210/148/7 - PB - 9781912710546 - Matt Lamination